Library Service to Children

A Guide to the Research, Planning, and Policy Literature

Phyllis Van Orden

American Library Association
Chicago and London 1992

Cover and text design by Dianne Rooney

Composed by Digital Graphics, Inc. in Stone Serif using TEX.
    Reproduction copy set on a Varityper 4300P phototypesetter

Printed on 50-pound Glatfelter, a pH-neutral stock, and bound in C1S
cover stock by McNaughton-Gunn

The paper used in this publication meets the minimum requirements of
American National Standard for Information Sciences—Permanence of
Paper for Printed Library Materials, ANSI Z39.48-1984. ∞

Library of Congress Cataloging-in-Publication Data
Van Orden, Phyllis.
    Library service to children : a guide to the research, planning,
and policy literature / by Phyllis Van Orden.
        p.   cm.
    Includes index.
    ISBN 0-8389-0584-6
    1. Libraries, Children's—Bibliography. 2. Children—Books and
reading—Bibliography. 3. Library science—Bibliography.
I. Title.
Z718.1.V336   1992   92-3823
016.02762'5—dc20

Contents

Acknowledgments

This work was made possible by a Whitney-Carnegie Grant from the American Library Association's Publishing Committee. The committee's action provided the funds to support the online searching and graduate assistance needed.

Colleagues across North America offered guidance in the design of the content and format of the text and index, as well as assistance in identifying specific items for consideration. Personnel from the American Library Association who offered support include Charles Harmon, librarian of the Headquarters Library; Susan Roman, executive director of the Association for Library Service to Children; and Herbert Bloom, senior editor of ALA Books.

The interlibrary loan department staff of Strozier Library, Florida State University, effectively responded to all the interlibrary loan requests and was helpful in locating evasive items.

The School of Library Science and Information Studies supported the project in a number of ways, including covering some of the postage and telephone costs. A number of students at the school participated in creating the bibliography. Special thanks go to Susan Higgins, who helped locate items and made interlibrary loan requests; to Kay Bishop, who handled the online searching and verification; and to Daniel Schiefelbein, who served as my graduate assistant during the 1990–1991 calendar year, conducted the

Multiple Use MARC System (MUMS) online search, and helped in numerous ways.

To each of these individuals and groups I owe a note of appreciation for their support and their belief in the value of this bibliography.

Introduction

Purpose

This annotated bibliography is designed to facilitate the location of English-language materials about public library services to children and children's librarianship (role and education), as addressed in goal statements, conference proceedings, policy literature, reports, and research studies.

Intended Audience

Researchers, agencies funding programs and research, state library consultants, children's services system coordinators, library educators, and other interested individuals or groups responsible for planning, evaluating, and educating children's librarians will find in the bibliography items to assist them.

Scope

The focus of the bibliography is on policy literature, historical works, research studies, reports, and conference proceedings relating to public library services to children and children's librarianship.

Works from the turn of the century are included; an analysis of these writings provides a record of the evolving place of children's services in public libraries and the changing role of children's librarians. Position statements and textbooks are included for their statements about goals of library services to children and their identification of the educational needs of children's librarians.

Information about key figures can be found in the following types of entries: biographies, works honoring these individuals, and histories of children's services.

All items in the bibliography are available through interlibrary loan or through purchase (information about how to obtain such items is included).

Type of Literature Included

The forms of literature represented in the bibliography include annual reports, biographies, bibliographies, directories, conference and institute proceedings, reports, research studies, guidelines, standards, and policies.

Evaluation reports include ones on Library Services and Construction Act (LSCA), Title IIB, and other pertinent funded projects. Research studies include books, dissertations, master's theses, statistical reports, and reports of projects. Canadian-based research studies are included when their findings have relevance to programs in the United States.

Guidelines and standards include those issued by national organizations, state library associations, and state agencies. Policies include separate documents, as well as ones reprinted in articles from library systems and associations. The majority of the documents are issued by United States federal, state, and municipal agencies and institutes; by national and state associations; and by individuals.

Value of the Work

The unique quality of the bibliography is its inclusion of policy statements, reports, and research studies not readily identified in any other one source. The following situations describe some of the ways the bibliography can aid library planners and researchers.

1. Library systems developing policy statements can access ten items under the heading "Libraries, Children's—Policies," including statements developed by professional associations and ones being used in several systems.
2. Professional groups developing guidelines for children's services in their areas will find existing documents listed under the headings "Libraries, Children's—Guidelines" and "Libraries, Children's—Standards."
3. Children's librarians can find discussions on how to write goals and objectives, as well as actual statements used in other systems.
4. Those responsible for in-service and preservice programs for children's librarians will find a range of opinion pieces and research under the subject heading "Librarians, Children's—Education."
5. Researchers can use the appendixes to identify works using different research methods, as well as funding sources that have been supportive of earlier research efforts.

Exclusions

Book lists, how-to-do-it activities and programming guides, research studies about juvenile literature, and nonresearch articles are not included in the bibliography. Research studies about library systems which group children's services with other services are also excluded.

Limitations

Works identified after July 1, 1991, and not immediately available through interlibrary loan are not included in the bibliography. These works include a number of master's theses cited in other research reports reviewed, as well as state association and state agency documents identified in correspondence received after July 1, 1991.

Sources Used to Identify Possible Entries

Items were identified using (1) manual searches, (2) online searches, and (3) letters to state library associations and state library consultants.

1. *Manual searches*: Five useful bibliographies are:
    Fitzgibbons, Shirley. "Research on Library Services for Children and Young Adults: Implications for Practices." *Emergency Librarian* 9:6–17 (May–June 1982).
    Gallivan, Marion F. "Research on Children's Services in Libraries." *Top of the News* 30:275–93 (April 1974).
    Lankford, Mary D. *Checklist of Library Resources Developed by State Education Agencies: An Annotated Bibliography.* Chicago: American Library Association, 1988.
    Shontz, Marilyn Louise. "Selected Research Related to Children's and Young Adult Services in Public Libraries." *Top of the News* 38:125–42 (Winter 1982).
    State Education Documents: A State-by-State Directory for Their Acquisition and Use. Chicago: American Library Association, 1989.
2. *Online searches:* Three online services were searched before July 1, 1991:
    Dialog One, using "children? ( ) librar?" and "public and child?" in the following files: Information Science ABS, Social SCI Search, ECER/EXCEP Child, NTIS, and LISA.
    Dissertation Abstracts, using "children? and librar?" and "public and child?" for the CD-ROM search and online.
    MUMS (Multiple Use MARC System), a subsystem of LOCIS (Library of Congress Information System), using "Libraries, Children's" and "Children's Librarians."
3. *Letters to associations and agencies:*
    State library associations were identified through their listing in the *ALA Handbook of Organization, 1989/1990* (Chicago: American Library Association).
    State library consultants were identified through their listing in the *Bowker Annual Library and Book Trade Almanac, 1990* (New York: R. R. Bowker).

Related Bibliographies and Sources

Users of the bibliography will want to consult *Children's Services in the American Public Library: A Selected Bibliography*, compiled by Fannette H. Thomas (Westport, Conn.: Greenwood Press, 1990), which covers the professional literature between 1876 and 1976 on a broader spectrum of the literature and includes more opinion pieces than this bibliography, with its emphasis on policy and research literature.

Readers interested in juvenile literature should consult *Children's Literature: A Guide to Reference Sources*, by Virginia Hamilton (Washington, D.C.: Library of Congress, 1966), and its supplements, which include book lists, general articles, and other information outside the scope of this bibliography.

Individuals seeking current state standards, statistics, and reports should consult the Headquarters Library of the American Library Association for its list of holdings. These materials can be obtained through interlibrary loan from the Headquarters Library and Information Center, American Library Association, 50 E. Huron St., Chicago, IL 60611, or individuals can contact Charles Harmon, librarian, at either 1-800-545-2433, extension 2153, or (312) 280-2153.

Entries

The bibliography's 298 numbered entries are arranged alphabetically by title, excluding "a," "an," and "the." Annotations include a description of the item, a listing of related entries, and purchasing information for materials available from state library associations. When a book is based on a dissertation, the title and bibliographic information for it are included. Descriptors include type of literature, funding source(s), research method(s), major professor if given in a dissertation or a Dissertation Abstract Index (DAI) abstract, statistical method(s), and subject heading(s). Bibliographic information varies depending on whether the entry is a dissertation, a book, an article, or a report.

SAMPLE ENTRIES

Dissertations

Bibliographic information for dissertations includes: title, author, degree, university, date, pagination, DAI number, and ED number if the dissertation is available through the ERIC Clearinghouse.

007 "An Analysis of Intermediate Grade Gifted Students and Their Book Experiences as Preschool Children" by Philip Ginneti. Ph.D. Diss., University of Akron, 1989. 162p. DAI 50/06A, p. 1614.

Analyzes the preschool experiences of 138 gifted and 92 nongifted children and the background information of their parents. Reports that (1) daily experiences with books help a child succeed in school; (2) gifted children's experiences include being read to daily, having books and reading areas in their homes, and going to the library more than once a month; and (3) parents of gifted children had higher levels of education and income. Concludes that primary caretakers influence a child's development from birth to age five and that their awareness of child development patterns is important in affecting the child's learning.

Type of literature:	Dissertation
Research method(s):	Questionnaire
Statistical method(s):	t test
Subject heading(s):	Children—Gifted
	Children—Preschoolers
	Reading

Books

Bibliographic information for books includes: title, author, series, edition, imprint, pagination, ISBN (International Standard Book Number), ISSN (International Standard Serial Number), and LCCN (Library of Congress Catalog Number).

016 *Apostles of Culture: The Public Librarian and American Society, 1876–1920* by Dee Garrison. New York: Free Press, 1979. 319p. ISBN 0-02-693850-2. LCCN 78-66979.

Describes how the role of domesticity imposed on working women created the early attention given to children's services. Notes the emphasis on recreational reading at the turn of the century, although the library had been conceived and theoretically maintained as an educational institution. Identifies the first mention of discipline problems occurring in the library literature of 1901.

        Type of literature: Book—Historical
        Subject heading(s):   Librarians, Children's—History
                                  Libraries, Children's—History

Periodical Articles

Bibliographic information for articles includes: title, author, journal, volume, pagination, month or season, and year.

022 "Beyond Shhh! Developing the Discipline Policy of the Downers Grove Public Library" by Christopher Bowen. *Illinois Libraries* 70:25–32 (Jan. 1988).

Includes the library's policies, which cover misconduct (noise level of conversation, running, harassing others, and fighting), eating, and drinking. Reports that (1) children younger than age six may not be left unattended, and (2) adults and minors may have their library privileges restricted for misconduct. Cites restriction period for minors as three months for the first offense and a year for the second.

        Type of literature: Article—Policy
        Subject heading(s):   Discipline—Policies
                                  Libraries, Children's—Discipline
                                  Libraries, Children's—Policies

Reports

Bibliographic information for reports includes: title, author, imprint, pagination, and ED (ERIC) number.

146　*An Investigation of the Effectiveness of an Online Catalog in Pro-viding Bibliographic Access to Children in a Public Library Set-ting. Research Report* by Leslie Edmonds, Paula Moore, and Kathleen Mehaffey Balcom. Champaign-Urbana: Graduate School of Library and Information Science, University of Illinois, 1989. 98p. ED 311–921.

Evaluates the use of an online catalog by children in comparison with their use of a card catalog. Reports on the testing of thirty-three children (fourth, sixth, and eighth grades) to determine whether they had the developmental skills needed to locate and interpret bibliographic information presented in both forms of the catalog. Reports that the children did not have a broad knowledge of alphabetizing or filing conventions and were able to successfully complete 65 percent of the card catalog searches and only 18 percent of the online searches. Calls for the development of software using natural language, fewer screens, and clearer help messages, and for library instruction to help children develop the necessary skills.

Type of literature:	Report—Research
Research method(s):	Observations; Interviews
Subject heading(s):	Libraries, Children's—Cataloging
	Libraries, Children's—User Studies

Appendixes

Descriptors used in the entries for research methods, funding sources, and types of literature were the basis for the listings in the appendixes. Appendix I lists the research methods used in the entries identified in the bibliography. Appendix II lists the sources of funding that supported the entries on research projects and the development of policy literature. Appendix III identifies the types of literature found in the 298 entries, including twenty-eight dissertations, three books based on dissertations, twelve master's theses, and one book based on a master's thesis.

Annotated Bibliography

001   *Advocating Access: Developing Community Library Services for Children and Young Adults in Washington State.* Children's and Young Adult Services (CAYAS), Washington Library Association, 1989. 46p.

Provides guidelines for developing library policies and procedures, planning documents, resources allocation, evaluation, services, collections, staffing, and facilities. Includes a "Philosophy of Youth Services," reading lists for planners, and appendixes with nationally endorsed documents.

Copies available for $10 each from CAYAS, Washington Library Association,1232 143rd Ave. SE, Bellevue, WA 98007.

Type of literature:	Guidelines
Subject heading(s):	Libraries, Children's—Administration and Organization—Washington State
	Libraries, Children's—Philosophy—Washington State

002 "ALA-Accredited Master's Degree: Considerations for Youth Services Librarianship" by Patsy H. Perritt and Kathleen M. Heim. *Top of the News* 43:149–59 (Winter 1987).
Contends that the ALA-accredited master's degree is the requisite credential for school and youth librarians. Recommends resolving the departmental location of educational preparation, developing standards for competencies and skills, and identifying and analyzing career paths for articulation and promotion.
        Type of literature: Article—Opinion
        Subject heading(s):   Librarians, Children's—
                                Education

003 *Alabama Public Library Service: 1988 Annual Report.* Montgomery: Alabama Public Library Service, 1988. 18p. ED 311 920.
Provides statistics about the summer reading program, including that at the Regional Library for the Blind and Physically Handicapped, whose patrons were provided materials in braille and recording formats.
    The *1987 Annual Report* (ED 297 783) includes a narrative report on children's services.
        Type of literature: Annual Report
        Subject heading(s):   Libraries, Children's—Statistics—
                                  Alabama

004 "ALSC's Goals and Objectives" by Phyllis Van Orden. *ALSC Newsletter* 7:1–2 (May 1986).
Reports the January 1986 actions of the board of the Association for Library Service to Children in adopting these guidelines for the association's long-range planning. Includes calls for collection and dissemination of information on the current status of library service to children, the appointment of a task force to identify the competencies needed by children's librarians, and the dissemination of information about existing and ongoing research concerning library service to children.
        Type of literature: Policies
        Subject heading(s):   Association for Library Service to Children—Goals and Objectives

005 "The American Origins of Public Library Work with Children" by Frances Clark Sayers. *Library Trends* 12:6–12 (July 1963).

Traces the development of children's services from apprentice libraries at the time of Benjamin Franklin to the children's rooms of the 1910s, noting the early and sustaining significance of book selection in children's services. Identifies the first American Library Association publication as John F. Sargent's *Reading for the Young* (1890).

Type of literature:	Article—Historical
Subject heading(s):	Libraries, Children's—History—United States

006 *The American Public Library* by Arthur E. Bostwick. 4th ed., rev. and enlarg. New York: D. Appleton, 1929. 471p. Illus. (photographs)

Describes the controversy over public libraries serving children. Identifies the special efforts to help children as taking four forms: (1) the children's corner, (2) the separate children's library, (3) the children's reading room, and (4) the children's room. Discusses the types of programs and services. Issued with the endorsement of the editorial committee of the American Library Association.

Type of literature:	Book—Opinion
Subject heading(s):	Libraries, Children's

007 "An Analysis of Intermediate Grade Gifted Students and Their Book Experiences as Preschool Children" by Philip Ginneti. Ph.D. Diss., University of Akron, 1989. 162p. DAI 50/06A, p. 1614.

Analyzes the preschool experiences of 138 gifted and 92 nongifted children and the background information of their parents. Reports that (1) daily experiences with books help a child succeed in school; (2) gifted children's experiences include being read to daily, having books and reading areas in their homes, and going to the library more than once a month; and (3) parents of gifted children had higher levels of education and income. Concludes that primary caretakers influence a child's development from birth to age five and that their awareness of child development patterns is important in affecting the child's learning.

Type of literature:	Dissertation
Research method(s):	Questionnaire
Statistical method(s):	t test
Subject heading(s):	Children—Gifted
	Children—Preschoolers
	Reading

008   "An Analysis of Reviews of Books of Fiction for Children
and Adolescents Published in Major Selection Aids in the
United States in 1979" by Phyllis Kay Kennemer. Ed.D. Diss.,
University of Colorado at Boulder, 1980. 156p. DAI 42/01A,
p. 81.
Examines and compares the review policies, formats, types, and
lengths of reviews of *Booklist, Bulletin of the Center for Children's
Books, Horn Book Magazine, Kirkus Reviews, Publishers Weekly,* and
School Library Journal. Evaluates reviews of fiction works in terms of
the number of descriptive, analytical, and sociological items.

Type of literature:	Dissertation
Research method(s):	Reviews—Analysis
Research instruments:	Classification of Book Reviews
	Form
Subject heading(s):	Reviews and Reviewing

009   "An Analytical Study of the Criteria Used in the Selection
of Children's Films in the Boston Public Library System" by
Euclid J. Peltier. v. I and II. Master's Thesis, Boston University,
1954. 125p.
Concludes that there are "no significant differences between librarians and community film borrowers in their selection, subject preference, and use of children's films" (p. 104). Reports that "film services
and film selections are satisfactory for both groups" (p. 104). Notes
that the demand for children's films exceeds the supply. Calls for
children's librarians to serve on film selection committees and to
invite children to participate in the previewing process. Describes
the uses of films in programming and identifies problems, such as
the lack of quality films.

Type of literature:	Master's Thesis
Research method(s):	Questionnaire

Subject heading(s):   Libraries, Children's—Collections
                           Films
                           Boston Public Library

010 "An Analytical Study of the Recommendations of Early
         Childhood Education Authorities with Regard to the Role
         of the Public Library in Serving Children from Infancy to
         Six Years of Age" by Frances A. Smardo. Ph.D. Diss., North
         Texas State University, 1978. 181p. DAI 39/07A, p. 3898. ED
         150 222.
Develops guidelines in the areas of services, programs, materials,
physical facilities, and personnel for public libraries serving young
children. Guidelines are based on recommendations by early childhood education authorities. Recommends that library schools provide professional preparation and experiences in early childhood
education or child development.

Type of literature: Dissertation
Research method(s):   Questionnaire; Interviews
Subject heading(s):   Children—Early Childhood
                           Librarians, Children's—Education
                           Libraries, Children's—Services

011 *An Analytical Survey of Illinois Public Library Service to Children*
         by Selma Richardson. Springfield: Illinois State Library, 1978.
         345p.
Identifies the status of service, personnel involved with services,
number and types of services, collections, and physical facilities of
all libraries in the state. Reports on visits to thirty-two libraries selected for quality of service, geographical distribution, and size of
population served.
    Reports preliminary findings in "An Analytical Survey of Illinois
Public Library Services to Children: Selected Findings," *Illinois Libraries* 60:497–504 (May 1978).

Type of literature: Report—Research
Funding source(s):   Library Services and Construction
                           Act (LSCA)

Research method(s):   Questionnaire; Site visits
Subject heading(s):   Libraries, Children's—Illinois

5

012   *Anne Carroll Moore: A Biography* by Frances C. Sayers. New York: Atheneum, 1972. 304p. Illus. (photographs). Chronology. LCCN 72-78291.

Compares Anne Carroll Moore to artists like Isaac Stern, Arthur Rubinstein, and Picasso, noting that "she lived and moved beyond the prescribed condition of her art: children, books, and the utmost reach of the public library" (p. xi). Credits Moore as the "one person more than any other who gave shape and content to the new profession [children's librarians] to the greatest degree and in the fullest measure" (p. x). Traces Moore's life from her ancestry to her training, using many quotations from Moore's correspondence.

Type of literature:	Biography
Subject heading(s):	Librarians, Children's— Biographies
	Moore, Anne Carroll— Biographies

013   "Anne Carroll Moore: A Study of Her Work with Children's Libraries and Literature" by Nancy Meade Akers. Master's Thesis, Pratt Institute, 1951. 49p.

Highlights Moore's contributions to the development of children's literature and to library work with children, covering Moore's ten years as children's librarian at the Pratt Institute Free Library and her forty-five years with the New York Public Library. Notes that many aspects of today's services to children were initiated under Moore's leadership. Closes with Moore's caution to young children's librarians: "Always remember . . . that you are making memories" (p. 47).

Type of literature:	Master's Thesis
Research method(s):	Interviews
Subject heading(s):	Librarians, Children's— Biographies
	Moore, Anne Carroll— Biographies

014   *Annual Program. Library Services and Construction Act, 1989–1990*. Columbia: South Carolina State Library, 1989. 88p. ED 316 240.

6

Includes fiscal and project descriptions, including objectives, needs assessment, service groups, activities, libraries involved, costs, and evaluation of the services to children funded under the 1989–1990 LSCA.

    Type of literature: Annual Report
    Subject heading(s):   Libraries, Children's—Services—
        South Carolina
        Library Services and Construction
        Act—South Carolina

015   *Annual Report. Oklahoma Public Libraries in Communities and State Libraries, July 1, 1988–June 30, 1989.* Oklahoma City: Oklahoma Department of Libraries, Public Information Office [1989]. Unp.

Provides statistics regarding programs for school-age children by library system and for those in mental institutions.

    Type of literature: Annual Report
    Subject heading(s):   Libraries, Children's—Statistics—
        Oklahoma

016   *Apostles of Culture: The Public Librarian and American Society, 1876–1920* by Dee Garrison. New York: Free Press, 1979. 319p. ISBN 0-02-693850-2. LCCN 78-66979.

Describes how the role of domesticity imposed on working women created the early attention given to children's services. Notes the emphasis on recreational reading at the turn of the century, although the library had been conceived and theoretically maintained as an educational institution. Identifies the first mention of discipline problems in the library literature of 1901.

    Type of literature: Book—Historical
    Subject heading(s):   Librarians, Children's—History
        Libraries, Children's—History

017   "Are Librarians Prepared to Serve Young Children?" by Frances A. Smardo. *Journal of Education for Librarianship* 209:274–84 (Spring 1980).

Reviews research literature on the qualifications of public librarians who work with children younger than six years old. Reports on the Dallas Public Library 1977 Youth Delphi survey, which supports the literature calling for more extensive training. Observes that early childhood authorities recommend child development coursework and field experiences with young children.

Type of literature:	Article—Research
Research method(s):	Questionnaire; Interview
Subject heading(s):	Children—Early Childhood
	Librarians, Children's—
	Education

018   *Are We "There" Yet? Evaluating Library Collections, Reference Services, Programs, and Personnel* by Jane Robbins and Douglas Zweizig. Madison: School of Library and Information Studies, University of Wisconsin-Madison, 1988. 152p.
Reprints of tutorials: "Are We There Yet, Evaluating Library Collections, Reference Services, Programs, and Personnel," *American Libraries* 16–17:624–27; 724–27; 780–84; 32–36 (Oct. 1985–March 1986).

Type of literature:	Essays
Subject heading(s):	Libraries, Children's—Evaluation

019   "Attitudes of School and Public Librarians toward Combined Facilities" by Terry L. Weech. *Public Library Quarterly* 3:51–67 (Spring 1979).
Surveys Iowa school and public librarians and finds little difference in attitudes. Reports that a larger percentage of the Iowa librarians saw some advantage in combined facilities than did the librarians in the Toronto study "Combination School and Public Libraries: An Attitudinal Study," by L. J. Amey and R. J. Smith.

Type of literature:	Article—Research
Research method(s):	Questionnaire
Subject heading(s):	Attitude Studies
	School and Public Libraries

020   "Augusta Baker: Exponent of the Oral Art of Storytelling; Utilizing Video as a Medium" by Maxine Modell Merriman. Ph.D. Diss., Texas Woman's University, 1983. 257p. DAI 44/10a, p. 2917.
Analyzes the relationship between a storyteller's personality and style and the storyteller's selections. Examines the impact of a live

audience on the quality and effectiveness of telling stories. Provides a biographical sketch of Augusta Baker. Describes the procedural scenario of video tape, which can be used as a teaching and in-service training tool in children's librarianship.

Type of literature: Dissertation
Research method(s): Interviews
Subject heading(s): Baker, Augusta—Biographies
           Librarians, Children's—
            Biographies
           Storytelling
           Video Production

021 *Avenues to Excellence II; Standards for Public Libraries in Illinois.* Chicago: Illinois Library Association, 1989. 56p.

Identifies the common purpose for all Illinois public libraries: "To provide access to the universe of information, and especially that information which is of immediate relevance and interest, to the community it serves" (p. 4). Provides output measures and bibliographies for each section: structure and governance, finances, administration, library image, users and usage (children's services as specific population), reference services, personnel, materials, physical facilities, and the Illinois Library and Information Network (ILLINET) responsibilities. Includes a glossary and appendixes that provide quantitative recommendations for facilities and holdings.

Type of literature: Standards
Subject heading(s): Libraries—Standards—Illinois

022 "Beyond Shhh! Developing the Discipline Policy of the Downers Grove Public Library" by Christopher Bowen. *Illinois Libraries* 70:25–32 (Jan. 1988).

Includes the library's policies, which cover misconduct (noise level of conversation, running, harassing others, and fighting), eating, and drinking. Reports that (1) children younger than age six may not be left unattended, and (2) adults and minors may have their library privileges restricted for misconduct. Cites restriction period for minors as three months for the first offense and a year for the second.

Type of literature: Article—Policy
Subject heading(s): Disciplines—Policies

Libraries, Children's—Discipline
Libraries, Children's—Policies

023   *A Bibliography of Librarianship: Classified and Annotated Guide to the Library Literature of the World (Excluding Slavonic and Oriental Languages)* by Margaret Buton and Marion E. Vosburgh. London: Library Association, 1934. Reprint, University Microfilms, 1964. Unp.
Describes titles covering library work with children (reading, public libraries, school libraries, school and public library relations, storytelling, instruction in library use, and bibliographies), the training of librarians, and professional associations and conferences.

Type of literature:	Bibliography
Subject heading(s):	Librarians—Education—Bibliographies
	Libraries, Children's—Bibliographies

024   *Book Reading and Library Usage: A Study of Habits and Perceptions.* Princeton, N.J.: Gallup, 1978. 108p.
Reports on 1,515 telephone interviews with adults regarding the library habits of their family members. Includes the effect of television on children's reading, frequency of children's reading and library visits, and children's reading levels. Commissioned by the American Library Association.

Type of literature:	Book—Research
Funding source(s):	Baker and Taylor
Research method(s):	Interviews
Subject heading(s):	Libraries, Children's—User Studies
	Reading

025   *Book Selection and Intellectual Freedom* by LeRoy Charles Merritt. New York: H. W. Wilson, 1970. 100p. ISBN 0-8242-0420-4. LCCN 79-116998.
Discusses value theory and demand theory. Defines obscenity and pornography. Explains the rationale for having selection policies. Includes a sample policy for children's books, with sections addressing selection for specific age levels (preschool, elementary school, and

junior high school students) and specific areas (folk and fairy literature, human relations, religion, and sex). Discusses collection maintenance, the role of professional associations and state library agencies, and professional activities in support of intellectual freedom.

> Type of literature: Manual
> Subject heading(s):   Intellectual Freedom
>   Libraries, Children's—Materials
>   Libraries, Children's—Selection
>   Policies

026   "Books in Spanish for Young Readers in School and Public Libraries: A Survey of Practices and Attitudes" by Isabel Schon,
Kenneth D. Hopkins, Isabelle Main, and B. R. Hopkins. *Library and Information Science Research* 9:21–28 (Jan.–March
1987).
Reports that (1) more than half of the 423 respondents purchase
books in Spanish for children and young adults, (2) the circulation
of these materials constitutes a small percentage of the total circulation, (3) reviews are a key factor in selection, and (4) "more than
one-fourth of the librarians were of the opinion that funds should
not be used to acquire books in Spanish . . . because this is not in
the best educational interests of young Hispanics in the U.S." (p. 26).

> Type of literature: Article—Research
> Research method(s):   Questionnaire
> Subject heading(s):   Libraries, Children's—Materials—
>   Spanish

027   *Bowker Annual Library and Book Trade Almanac.* New York:
R. R. Bowker, 1956– . ISBN 0-8352-2943-2. ISSN 0068-0540.
LCCN 55-12434.
Lists accredited library schools; library scholarship sources; statistics
for salaries, library expenditures, price indexes, and library build-
ings; distinguished books; library and related organizations; professional books; and publishers' toll-free numbers.

> Type of literature: Almanac
> Subject heading(s):   Librarians—Salaries
>   Librarians—Scholarships

028 *The Canadian School-Housed Public Library*, ed. by L. J. Amey. Occasional Paper series, no. 24. Series Editor: Norman Horrocks. Halifax, Nova Scotia: Dalhousie University Libraries and Dalhousie School of Library Service, 1979. 488p. ISBN 0-7703-159-2.

Covers the history and legislation for 179 school-house public libraries by region and territory. Provides examples of agreements and floor plans. Includes a directory with names and addresses of libraries, names and types of schools, and other descriptive information.

Type of literature:	Report—Research
Research method(s):	Questionnaire; Interviews
Subject heading(s):	School and Public Libraries— Canada

029 *Caroline M. Hewins: Her Book* by Caroline M. Hewins. Boston: Horn Book, 1954. 107p. Illus. (plates)

Contains "A Mid-Century Child and Her Books," by Caroline M. Hewins, and "Caroline M. Hewins and Books for Children," by Jennie D. Lindquist. Highlights Hewins' development of library service in Hartford, Connecticut, and her contributions to the field.

Type of literature:	Biography
Subject heading(s):	Hewins, Caroline M.— Biographies Librarians, Children's— Biographies

030 "Carrying on the Tradition: Training Librarians for Children's Services" by Adele Fasick. In *Lands of Pleasure: Essays on Lillian H. Smith and the Development of Children's Libraries*, pp. 19–32, ed. by Adele M. Fasick, Margaret Johnston, and Ruth Osler. Metuchen, N.J.: Scarecrow Press, 1990.

Reviews the changes in library education for children's librarians for the last century. Notes changes in social climate (media, views of the child, family structure, educational patterns) and in public library services to children (toddler programs, mainstreaming). Calls for continuing education opportunities to address the future, stating that "education for children's librarians must reflect the social climate outside the library and take into account the new patterns which affect library services. . . . New skills are now needed as well as new ways of updating education to keep up with developments in society, technology, and libraries."

Type of literature: Essay—Opinion
Subject heading(s):   Librarians, Children's—Education

031   *The Central Children's Library in Metropolitan Public Libraries* by Mae Benne. Seattle: School of Librarianship, University of Washington, 1977. 80p.

Examines the roles and functions central to children's libraries in twenty-seven urban library systems in the United States and Canada. Focuses on the impact of changes in central cities, changes in administrative patterns, and priorities established in response to the financial problems that large urban centers faced in the 1970s.

Type of literature: Report—Research
Funding source(s):   Council on Library Resources
    Fellowship
    Professional Leave
Research method(s):   Interviews
Subject heading(s):   Libraries, Children's—
    Administration and
    Organization
    Libraries, Children's—
    Metropolitan

032   *The Changing Role in Children's Work in Public Libraries: Issues and Answers: A Post-Conference Report on a Pre-Conference Workshop, June 16, 1977.* Detroit, Mich.: Detroit Public Library, 1977. 35p. ED 156 129.

Includes Sara Innis Fenwick's history of children's librarianship, Mary Kingsburg's report on a Delphi study about trends, Mae Benne's preliminary report on the metropolitan libraries, and Margaret Mary Kimmel's call for research.

Type of literature: Conference Proceedings
Subject heading(s):   Libraries, Children's—
    Conferences and Institutes—
    Proceedings
    Libraries, Children's—History

Libraries, Children's—
Metropolitan
Libraries, Children's—Services

033   "Characteristics of Users and Nonusers of Elementary School
Library Services and Public Library Services for Children" by
Myriette Revenna Guinyard Ekechukwu. Ph.D. Diss., University of Washington, 1972. 216p. DAI 33/08A, p. 4443.
Describes 472 fifth-grade users and nonusers of school and public
library services in terms of sex, distance of residence from the library, mode of travel to the library, frequency of library use, reasons
for using or not using the library, and attitudes toward the library.
Reports significant relations between (1) mode of travel to the public library and frequency of use and (2) what children liked best or
disliked most about the public library and their use of it.

Type of literature:	Dissertation
Major professor:	Dianne L. Monson
Research method(s):	Questionnaire
Subject heading(s):	Libraries, Children's—User Studies

034   *Checklist of Library Resources Developed by State Education
Agencies: An Annotated Bibliography* by Mary D. Lankford. A
Publication of the American Association of School Libraries
(AASL) Publications Committee. Chicago: American Library
Association, 1988. 128p. ISBN 8389-7229-2.
Provides full bibliographic information, ordering information, de-
scriptive annotations from the cited works, and entries used in the
index (state, title, subject headings). Identifies documents covering
the role of school and public libraries, bibliographies, and other
guides.

Type of literature:	Bibliography
Subject heading(s):	State Education Agencies— Bibliographies

035   *Children in Libraries: Patterns of Access to Materials and Services in School and Public Libraries*, ed. by Zena Sutherland.
Proceedings of the Forty-first Conference of the Graduate

Library School, May 16–17, 1980. Chicago: University of Chicago Press, 1981. 89p. ISBN 0-226-78063-5.
Focuses on "children's social rights, their rights to equal educational opportunities, and their legal rights, especially when those rights are denied or abridged by their guardians or by society" (p. 1). Examines access from several perspectives: individual libraries, library systems, interlibrary loan programs, international publishing, roles of writers and reviewers, and censorship.

Related entries: "Children's Access to Public Library Services: Prince George's County Memorial Public Library, Maryland, 1980," by Lillian N. Gerhardt, and "Children's Access to Library Systems," by Marilyn Miller.

Also available as a theme issue in *Library Quarterly* 51 (Jan. 1981).

Type of literature:	Conference Proceedings
Subject heading(s):	Access
	Libraries, Children's—
	Conferences and Institutes—
	Proceedings

036 *Children Using Media: Reading and Viewing Preferences among the Users and Non-Users of the Regina Public Library* by Adele M. Fasick and Claire England. Prepared by the Centre for the Regina Public Library, Regina, Saskatchewan, Canada. Toronto: Centre for Research in Librarianship, Faculty of Library Science, University of Toronto, 1977. 79p.

Interviews 540 children (ages six to twelve) in the library and 260 in the schools to ascertain their purpose in using the library and how well their informational and recreational needs were met. Uses the Piers-Harris Self Concept Scale to measure the children's feelings of competence and self-worth. Analyzes different characteristics of the users and nonusers. Recommends changes in policies, planning, collections, services, programs, and publicity.

Type of literature:	Report—Research
Research method(s):	Interviews; Collection Analysis; Circulation Records—Analysis
Statistical method(s):	Statistical Package for the Social Sciences
Subject heading(s):	Libraries, Children's—User Studies

037   "Children's Access to Information in Print: An Analysis of
the Vocabulary (Reading) Levels of Subject Headings and
Their Application" by Joy Kaiser Moll. Ph.D. Diss., Rutgers
University, 1975. 162p. DAI 36/02A, p. 586.
Compares reading levels for Library of Congress (LC) 7.7, Sears 6.9,
MARC 6.4, and LC Junior 6.0. Identifies problems for children due
to vocabulary level, inconsistent form of headings, and mismatch
of conceptual patterns. Finds no relationship between the vocabulary level of subject headings and the readability level of books the
headings describe.

Type of literature:	Dissertation
Research method(s):	Subject Headings—Analysis
Subject heading(s):	Libraries, Children's—Cataloging
	Libraries, Children's—Subject Headings

038   "Children's Access to Library Systems" by Marilyn Miller. See
Children in Libraries (035).
Reports on an unpublished study of access to children's materials
through inter- and intra-loan policies and procedures conducted
by a committee of the Association for Library Service to Children
(ALSC) in 1977. Notes that those libraries whose interlibrary loan
(ILL) policies followed the code of ALA limit loans to serious re-
searchers; thus, children were not allowed to use this service.

Type of literature:	Article—Research
Research method(s):	Questionnaire
Subject heading(s):	Access
	Interlibrary Loan

039   "Children's Access to Public Library Services: Prince George's
County Memorial Public Library, Maryland, 1980" by Lillian
N. Gerhardt. See *Children in Libraries* (035).
Examines the library's publicity, transportation, scheduling, ar-
chitecture, location of materials, storage, budget, openness of col-
lections, ILL, extension services, and relations with schools.

Type of literature:	Article—Research
Research method(s):	Interviews
Subject heading(s):	Access
	Interlibrary Loan

Libraries, Children's—Policies
Libraries, Children's—Services

040 "Children's Librarianship: A Descriptive Study of the Responsibilities Found in Job Announcements and Written Job Descriptions, Compared with Perceptions of Successful Applicants" by Catherine Howard. Ph.D. Diss., Indiana University, 1989. 187p. DAI 50/05A, p. 1123.
Compares job announcements and descriptions with the perceived importance of successful applicants for those positions. Reports discrepancies in a number of areas. Finds collection development, reference and readers advisory functions, and programming high on the list of job responsibilities. Identifies library instruction and toddler programs as the most important types of programs.

Type of literature:	Dissertation
Major professor:	Shirley Fitzgibbons
Research method(s):	Job Announcements—Analysis; Questionnaire
Subject heading(s):	Librarians, Children's—Education
	Librarians, Children's—Job Announcements
	Librarians, Children's—Job Descriptions

041 "Children's Librarianship: The Unmet Personnel Needs" by Shirley Fitzgibbons. *New Jersey Libraries* 16:8–17 (Fall 1983).
Reviews literature dealing with children's librarians' feeling of low status. Analyzes job advertisements in *American Libraries* for 1982 and the first half of 1983 in terms of openings and skills needed for children's, young adult, and youth librarians.

Type of literature:	Article—Research
Research method(s):	Job Announcements—Analysis
Subject heading(s):	Librarians, Children's—Job Announcements

042 "Children's Libraries: Nineteen Century American Origins" by Manuel D. Lopez. *Journal of Library History, Philosophy, and Comparative Librarianship* 11:316–42 (Oct. 1976).

Traces the development of children's services from the 1850s to 1900, describing the professional leaders and the services they provided for children. Describes the social conditions and developing role of children's libraries.

    Type of literature: Article—Historical
    Subject heading(s):   Libraries, Children's—History—
                               United States

043   "Children's Libraries and Librarianship" by Florence W. Butler. In *Encyclopedia of Library and Information Science*, v. 4, pp. 559–66. New York: Marcel Dekker, 1970. LCCN 68-31232.

Traces the development of children's services in the United States, including the early leaders, the role of professional organizations, and international ties.

    Type of literature: Essay—Historical
    Subject heading(s):   Libraries, Children's—History—
                               United States

044   *The Children's Library: A Dynamic Factor in Education* by Sophy H. Powell, with an introduction by John Cotton Dana. New York: H. W. Wilson, 1917. 460p.

Discusses trends and issues of the period, giving historical background. Raises questions for the children's room: (1) "Does the children's room as an educational factor rest upon some social and economic needs?" (2) "Is it conducted according to psychological principles?" (3) "Is there a definite idea of the ends to be served by the separate department?" and (4) "Is there an approximately accurate measure of accomplishment?" Addresses educational needs of children's librarians. Provides an extensive bibliography, pages 341 to 456.

    Type of literature: Book—Historical
    Subject heading(s):   Librarians, Children's—
                               Education
                               Libraries, Children's—History—
                               United States

045 *Children's Library Services Handbook* by Jane Gardner Connor. Phoenix, Ariz.: Oryx Press, 1960. 128p. Illus. (photographs). ISBN 0-89774-489-6. LCCN 89-8569.

Addresses the whys and hows of service to children. Includes sample job descriptions. Based on the Children's Services Handbook (unpublished LSCA project, 1985) by the author as field service librarian for children's services at the South Carolina State Library.

Type of literature:	Manual
Subject heading(s):	Libraries, Children's— Administration and Organization
	Librarians, Children's—Job Descriptions

046 *Children's Library Yearbook* by the Committee on Library Work with Children, American Library Association. Chicago: American Library Association, 1929–1932. Illus. LCCN 29-12747. Number one, 1929, p. 130; Number two, 1930, p. 88; Number three, 1931, p. 80; and Number four, 1932, p. 191.

Number one covers the history of children's services and organization. Number four addresses services for special groups: Indian, Negro. The appendixes in all four volumes include bibliographies, salary statistics, and a directory of children's librarians who were members of the ALA.

Type of literature:	Yearbook
Subject heading(s):	Librarians, Children's— Directories
	Libraries, Children's—Yearbooks

047 *Children's Literature: A Guide to Reference Sources* by Virginia Haviland. Washington, D.C.: Library of Congress, 1966. 342p. *First Supplement,* 1971. 316p. *Second Supplement,* 1977. 413p.

Provide annotations describing books, articles, and pamphlets primarily on children's literature. "The Library and Children's Books" section lists standards and other basic works about services to children.

Type of literature:	Bibliography

Subject heading(s):   Libraries, Children's—
                                    Bibliographies
                              Literature, Children's—
                                    Bibliographies

048   "Children's Reference Services Survey" by the Canadian Association of Children's Librarians (CACL) Committee on Reference Materials for Children. *Canadian Library Journal* 41:16–18 (Feb. 1984).

Reports on the use of the public library (Calgary) by 1,635 children in grades four, five, and six, and identifies the questions they asked most often. Surveys library staff in thirteen branches to ascertain how children ask questions and how well library collections meet the needs of the users. Calls for reference staff to have knowledge of children's reading levels, for children's services staff to have training in reference, and for those involved in reference work with children to participate in selecting the reference materials they use.

        Type of literature: Article—Research
        Research method(s):   Questionnaire
        Subject heading(s):   Libraries, Children's—Reference
                                    Service

049   *Children's Service in Public Libraries: Organization and Administration* by Elizabeth Henry Gross, with the collaboration of Gener Inyart Hamovicz. Chicago: American Library Association, 1963. 124p.

Supplements the *Public Library Inquiry* by examining the types of organization, services given, prevailing policies, and means by which objectives for children's services were being met in 1957–58. Reports responses from both the administrators and the children's supervisors. Uses five groups of libraries, from one serving populations as small as 3,500 to one serving more than 100,000.

        Type of literature: Book—Research
        Funding source(s):   Old Dominion Foundation,
                                    Incorporated
        Research method(s):   Questionnaire; Interviews; Site
                                    visits

Subject heading(s):   Libraries, Children's—
                           Administration and
                           Organization

050   *Children's Services in a Small Public Library* by Winifred Rags-
          dale. Small Libraries Project series, no. 12. [Chicago]: Amer-
          ican Library Association, Library Administration Division,
          1967. 12p.
Provides guidelines for establishing and operating children's services, including the collection, a reader's advisory service, and reference material.
          Type of literature: Guidelines
          Subject heading(s):   Libraries, Children's—Guidelines

051   "Children's Services in California Public Libraries" by Robert
          Grover and Mary Kevin Moore. Los Angeles: School of Li-
          brary and Information Management, University of Southern
          California, [1981]. 34p.
Assesses the level of services to children to determine the extent to
which libraries were meeting the 1979 California guidelines in terms
of staffing, the educational background of children's librarians, collections, the use of selection tools, the physical facility, and services.
Recommends coursework needed, adding nonprint materials to collections, and other ways to strengthen children's services.
          Type of literature: Report—Research
          Funding source(s):   California Library Association,
                                        Children's Services Chapter
          Research method(s):   Questionnaire
          Subject heading(s):   Librarians, Children's—
                                        Education
                                     Libraries, Children's—Services—
                                        California

052   *Children's Services in Public Libraries: Research and Assessment
          for Michigan* by Julie Beth Todaro, Marcia Anolik Shafer, and
          Carole J. McCollough. Lansing: Children's Services Division,
          Michigan Library Association, 1985. 87p.

21

Establishes baseline data against which libraries could compare their programs in terms of library characteristics, services provided, facilities, collections, policies, and procedures.

Type of literature:	Report—Research
Funding source(s):	Michigan Educational Foundation
	Michigan Library Association
Research method(s):	Questionnaire
Subject heading(s):	Libraries, Children's—Services—Michigan

053 *Children's Services in the American Public Library: A Selected Bibliography*, compiled by Fannette H. Thomas. Bibliographies and Indexes in Library and Information Science series. Westport, Conn.: Greenwood Press, 1990. 151p. ISBN 0-313-24721-8. ISSN 0742-6879. LCCN 90-40197.
Provides descriptive annotations for professional literature published between 1876 and 1976 that address the major developments, trends, innovations, and practices. Organizes by historical focus, professional staff, organization scheme, philosophical perspective, client group, collection development, readers' services, story hours, interagency cooperation, and multimedia.

Type of literature:	Bibliography
Subject heading(s):	Libraries, Children's—Bibliographies

054 *Children's Services Manual*, ed. by Linda Boyles and Roseanne Russo. Tallahassee: Florida Department of State, Division of Library and Information Services, State Library of Florida, 1988. 75p.
Includes sample policies, such as the "Tampa-Hillsborough County Public Library System Materials Selection Policy," sample goal statements, and forms used by libraries throughout the state of Florida.

Type of literature:	Guidelines
Funding source(s):	State Library of Florida
Subject heading(s):	Libraries, Children's—Guidelines—Florida
	Libraries, Children's—Policies—Florida

055 *Children's Services of Public Libraries*, ed. by Selma K. Richard-
son. Papers presented at the Allerton Park Institute, spon-
sored by the University of Illinois Graduate School of Li-
brary Science, held November 13–16, 1977, Allerton House,
Monticello, Illinois. Allerton Park Institute series, no. 23.
Champaign-Urbana: Graduate School of Library Science,
University of Illinois, 1978. 178p. ISBN 0-87845-049-1.
LCCN 78-11503.
Includes presentations addressing children's services from a num-
ber of perspectives. Peggy A. Sullivan, in "Goals of Public Library
Services for Children," pages 1 to 8, addresses the personality of
children's librarians and calls for means of measuring the accom-
plishment of goals. Sullivan's speech is reprinted as "Deja Vu from
the Bridge" in *School Library Journal* 25:19–23 (April 1979).
   For the research perspective, see Mary E. Kingsbury's "Keeping
Out of Trouble" (150).

Type of literature:	Conference Proceedings
Subject heading(s):	Libraries, Children's—
	Conferences and Institutes—
	Proceedings
	Libraries, Children's—Goals and
	Objectives

056 "Classroom Orientation to the Use of the Public Library
and Its Effect on Fifth and Sixth Grade Students" by Leslie
Edmonds. Ph.D. Diss., Loyola University of Chicago, 1984.
319p. DAI 45/01A, p. 68.
Measures patterns of student use of the public library and explores
whether those patterns could be modified by implementing a program designed to encourage library use. Concludes that students
need to understand what library services are available and that librarians should work with teachers, who influence students in their
use of the library.

Type of literature:	Dissertation
Major professor:	Mary Jane Gray
Research method(s):	Quasi-experimental; Question-
	naire; Observation
Statistical method(s):	Statistical Package for the Social
	Sciences

Subject heading(s):   Libraries, Children's—User's
                             Studies

057   "Combination School and Public Libraries: An Attitudinal
           Study" by L. J. Amey and R. J. Smith. *Canadian Library Journal*
           33:251–61 (June 1976).
Identifies potential areas of conflict between high school librarians
and public librarians in Toronto regarding location, economy, operations, collection, and roles of combined facilities.
           Type of literature: Article—Research
           Research method(s):   Questionnaire
           Subject heading(s):   Attitude Studies
                                        School and Public Libraries

058   "The Combination School and Public Library: A Bibliogra-
           phy with Special Emphasis on the Canadian Experience" by
           L. J. Amey. *Canadian Library Journal* 33:263–67 (June 1976).
Includes provincial and other surveys of library service, reports, and
newspaper stories.
           Type of literature: Bibliography
           Subject heading(s):   School and Public Libraries—
                                        Bibliographies

059   *Combined School/Public Libraries: A Survey with Conclusions
           and Recommendations* by Wilma Lee Broughton Woolard.
           Metuchen, N.J.: Scarecrow Press, 1980. 184p. ISBN 0-8108-
           1335-1. LCCN 80-36742.
Identifies preexisting conditions within schools and communities
conducive to combining, staffing, governance, advantages, and limitations. Identifies unique or exemplary programs and operations in
the United States, and includes sample contracts and policies. Provides annotated bibliography on pages 83 to 102. Based on a revision
of Woolard's master's thesis.
           Type of literature: Book—Research
           Research method(s):   Questionnaire
           Subject heading(s):   School and Public Libraries

060 "Community Library Services—Working Papers on Goals and Guidelines" by the Task Force of the Standards Committee, Public Library Association. *School Library Journal* 20:21–27 (Sept. 1973).

Presents working documents for use in continuing deliberations on community library services. Provides working papers on goals and objectives for adult services, young adult services, and children's services. Identifies goals for children's services, including providing opportunities for children to (1) expand their knowledge, (2) further their search for an understanding of themselves and their environment, (3) satisfy their need for aesthetic experiences, (4) develop pride in their heritages and an appreciation of other cultures, (5) improve their ability to make critical judgments, and (6) develop their verbal, visual, and aural communication skills.

Type of literature: Guidelines
Subject heading(s): Libraries, Children's—Guidelines

061 "A Comparative Analysis of Juvenile Book Review Media" by Virginia Witucke. *School Media Quarterly* 8:153–60 (Spring 1980).

Examines the contents, policies, handling of reviews (coverage, promptness), and characteristics of reviews (length, authorship, critical themes, consistency) of five major review sources for juvenile books in terms of their coverage of thirty titles chosen from the 1972, 1973, and 1974 lists of Notable Children's Books. Calls for increased coverage, publication of reviewing journal's policy statement, promptness, and provision of subject access.

Type of literature: Article—Research
Research method(s): Reviews—Analysis
Subject heading(s): Reviews and Reviewing

062 "A Comparative Analysis of Public Library Service to Children in Indiana during the 1970s" by Barbara Kasper. Ph.D. Diss., Indiana University, 1985. 188p. DAI 46/10A, p. 2844.

Analyzes children's services, socioeconomic conditions, and adult services. Reports that professional staff serving children provide programs, activities, and services recommended at the national level, almost double the statewide mean. Finds that high-level services for both adults and children were found in the same libraries. Compares findings with ones on children's services in Wisconsin, Ohio, and Illinois.

Type of literature:	Dissertation
Research method(s):	Questionnaire
Subject heading(s):	Libraries, Children's—Services—Indiana

063   "A Comparative Study of Subject Headings for Children's Materials" by Thera P. Cavender. *Journal of Cataloging and Classification* 11:13–28 (Jan. 1955).

Compares Sears with Eloise Rue and Effie LaPlante's *Subject Headings for Children's Materials*, noting variations, coverage, generic versus specific wording, singular and plural forms, use of hyphens, and capitalization. Describes which authority would meet the needs of different-sized libraries.

Type of literature:	Article—Research
Research method(s):	Subject Headings—Analysis
Subject heading(s):	Libraries, Children's—Cataloging

064   "A Comparison of Children's Collections in Public and Elementary School Libraries" by Carol A. Doll. *Collection Management* 7:41–59 (Spring 1985).

Uses four Illinois communities and two in South Carolina to identify overlap in informational and recreational books. Reports that (1) schools have more informational and audiovisual materials, (2) public libraries have more story records, and (3) these complementary collections can serve as a basis for resource sharing.

Type of literature:	Article—Research
Research method(s):	Site visits; Questionnaire; Collection Analysis
Subject heading(s):	Libraries, Children's—Collections Libraries, School—Collections

065   "A Comparison of the Impact of Three Methods of Storyhour Presentation upon Children's Listening Skills" by Frances A. Smardo. *Public Library Quarterly* 4:33–42 (Spring 1983).

Reports on the effectiveness of three types of public library story hour programs (live, 16mm commercially produced film, video taped) in the acquisition of receptive language (listening skills) of children three, four, and five years of age. Finds that Head Start children need organized story hours to develop listening skills.

Also available: Monograph of the research for purchase; slide/tape for loan from author.

Type of literature:	Article—Research
Research method(s):	Experimental
Research instrument(s):	*Test of Basic Experiences (TOBE) 2, Language*
Subject heading(s):	Libraries, Children's—Programs and Activities
	Storyhours

066 "A Comparison of the Use Made of the Public Library and the School Library by Elementary School Students" by Blanche E. Janecek. Master's Thesis, University of Chicago, 1949. 160p.

Compares (1) the use made of school and public libraries by children (eight to thirteen years old), (2) the extent of duplication of materials, and (3) the similarities and variations in services in four communities in the city of Chicago. Reports that (1) uses made were similar,(2) duplication did not exist to a great extent, and (3) accessibility was a key factor for use.

Type of literature:	Master's Thesis
Research method(s):	Questionnaire
Subject heading(s):	Libraries, Children's—User Studies

067 "Competencies for Librarians Serving Children in Public Libraries" by the Association for Library Service to Children, a division of the American Library Association. Chicago: The Association, c1989. Brochure. ISSN 0-8378-7360-4.

Recommends competencies based on the belief that the "philosophical basis for children's services in public libraries is full access for children to library materials and services." Competencies are grouped by (1) knowledge of client group, (2) administrative and management skills, (3) communication skills, (4) materials and collection development, (5) programming skills, (6) advocacy, public

relations, and networking skills, and (7) professionalism and professional development. Adopted by the Board of Directors on January
10, 1989.

Copies available for $2 from ALSC/ALA, 50 E. Huron St., Chicago,
IL 60611.

Draft version available in *ALSC Newsletter* 9:3–4 (May 1988). ISSN
0162-6612. Excerpt in *Journal of Youth Services* 2:219–23 (Spring
1989). Also available as "Competencies for Librarians Serving Children in Public Libraries," *Journal of Youth Services in Libraries* 2: 219–
23 (Spring 1989).

Type of literature:	Guidelines
Subject heading(s):	Librarians, Children's— Competencies

068 "Competencies for Youth Services Libraries" by the Youth
Services Advisory Committee to the North Carolina State
Library, North Carolina Department of Cultural Resources.
Raleigh: North Carolina Department of Cultural Resources,
Division of State Library, 1988. Sections I–X. Three-hole
punched.

Identifies competencies in knowledge of library policies, procedures,
and goals; youth services department goals and objectives; client
group; library materials; collection development and maintenance;
programming; publicity and public relations; interpersonal relations; and professional development. Rates each competency in
terms of level of position and educational background of personnel and offers suggestions and information to help one meet those
competencies.

Type of literature:	Manual
Funding source(s):	Library Services and Construction Act, Title I
Subject heading(s):	Librarians, Children's— Competencies

069 "Competencies of Children's Librarians: An Attitudinal Assessment" by Julie Beth Todaro. D.L.S. Diss., Columbia University, 1984. 337p. DAI 46/03A, p. 544.

Compares the attitudes of public library directors, children's librarians, and library educators toward about forty-five competencies.

Identifies three types of competencies (knowledge, skills and abilities, and attitudes) covering seven subject areas: administration, materials, programmatic, audience and child, community, institutional, and professional. Concludes that the respondents want children's librarians to be specialists at a time when the literature is calling for generalists.

Type of literature:	Dissertation
Major professor:	Jane Anne Hannigan
Research method(s):	Questionnaire
Statistical method(s):	Multiple Classification Analysis
Subject heading(s):	Attitude Studies
	Librarians, Children's—
	Competencies

070 "Connecticut Libraries Survey: Children's Services Lacking." *Library Journal* 98:2597–98 (Sept. 15, 1973).

Reports the major findings of a 1972 survey of public libraries and branches regarding staff, materials, and services conducted by Faith H. Hektoen, Connecticut State Library consultant to children and young adults. Finds that (1) 108 of the 169 public libraries had designated children's librarians, of whom forty-two had library science degrees, and (2) children's materials had been allocated 10 to 14 percent of each library's budget.

Type of literature:	Article—Research
Research method(s):	Questionnaire
Subject heading(s):	Libraries, Children's—
	Connecticut

071 "The Connecticut Research Documentation Project" by Faith H. Hektoen. *School Library Journal* 26:20–24 (April 1980).

Describes the conception, criteria used for selection of participants, data collection and analysis, and findings of the Research Documentation Project (RDP), which was designed to collect measurements of children's services by participating libraries. Provides the form used for data collection. Describes the meetings of the participants and identifies the benefits of the project. Reports that the results include the documentation of the adult use of children's services.

Finds that information from the project helped local libraries and the state library in planning.

Complete report is available: *The Connecticut Research Documentation Project in Children's Service,* v. I and II, by Faith H. Hektoen (Hartford: Connecticut State Library, 1981).

Type of literature:	Article—Research
Research method(s):	Services Requested—Analysis
Subject heading(s):	Librarians, Children's—Inservice Education
	Libraries, Children's—Services—Connecticut

072 *Considerations before Writing a Public Library Building Program in Children's Services* by the Connecticut Environments for Children Committee. Hartford: Connecticut State Library, 1978. ED 207 570.

Identifies behaviors observed in children's rooms, provides an audiovisual philosophy statement, and identifies materials and areas needs.

Type of literature:	Guidelines
Subject heading(s):	Libraries, Children's—Facilities—Guidelines

073 "A Contemplation of Children's Services in Public Libraries of Wisconsin" by Helen Kreigh. *Public Library Quarterly* 20:57–59 (Summer 1981).

Describes the charges to a statewide planning committee and identifies the questions they hope to address. Reports on a survey of ratings of state consultant services and the lack of knowledge of such services.

Type of literature:	Article—Planning
Research method(s):	Questionnaire
Subject heading(s):	Libraries, Children's—Administration and Organization—Wisconsin
	Libraries, State—Services

074 "A Content Analysis of Children's Picture Story Book Reviews Published in Selected Journals during the Year 1981" by Janelle S. Dodson. Ph.D. Diss., Southern Illinois University, 1983. 135p. DAI 44/05A, p. 1361.

Examines 625 reviews in the 1981 issues of *Booklist, Bulletin of the Center for Children's Books, Horn Book Magazine,* and *School Library Journal* in terms of the descriptive and evaluative information about textual and visual aspects of the books.

Type of literature:	Dissertation
Research method(s):	Reviews—Analysis
Subject heading(s):	Reviews and Reviewing

075 "Continuing Education for the Personnel of Small Public Libraries: Program Development at the Iowa State University Library and Its Public Services Course" by Diana D. Shonrock. Iowa State University Library Series in Continuing Education, no. 2. Ames: Iowa State University of Science and Technology, 1983. 20p. ED 265 885.

Describes the planning, implementation, and evaluation of a staff development program for certified, nondegree credit for nonprofessional librarians. Includes five three-hour sessions on reference interviews, interlibrary loan, government publications, statistical tools, circulation, media services, and children's literature. Calls for more information about programming for upper elementary grade students.

Type of literature:	Report—Institutes
Subject heading(s):	Librarians, Children's—
	Education

076 *Cooperation between Types of Libraries 1940–1968: An Annotated Bibliography* by Ralph H. Stenstrom. Chicago: American Library Association, 1970. 159p. ISBN 0-8389-0094-1. LCCN 71-140212.

Describes articles about the nature of cooperative projects and the types of libraries (public school, academic-research, and special) involved. Arranges entries chronologically.

Type of literature:	Bibliography
Subject heading(s):	Libraries—Cooperation—
	Bibliographies
	School and Public Libraries—
	Bibliographies

077   *Cooperation in Library Service to Children* by Esther R. Dyer.
            Metuchen, N.J.: Scarecrow Press, 1978. 152p. ISBN 0-8108-
            1111-1.
Concludes that "cooperation between school and public library services to children is not expected to be a priority program in either
institution, nor is it likely to become a policy function at the board
level. The abstract ideal of cooperation is reinforced, but the plausi-
bility of actual implementation seems extremely dubious" (p. 212).
    Based on Dyer's dissertation, "Cooperation in Library Service to
Children: A Fifteen-Year Forecast of Alternatives Using the Delphi
Technique." D.L.S. Diss., Columbia University, 1976. 364p. DAI
39104A, p. 1904.

Type of literature:	Book—Research
Funding source(s):	Tangley Oaks Fellowship
Research method(s):	Delphi
Subject heading(s):	Libraries—Cooperation

078   "Cooperative Library Services to Children in Public Libraries
            and Public School Systems in Selected Communities in In-
            diana" by Esther Blanche Woolls. Ph.D. Diss., Indiana Uni-
            versity, 1972. 241p. DAI 34/03A, p. 1304.
Describes methods of communication, cooperative activities, and
joint services between public and school libraries. Identifies barriers
for such efforts as lack of communication, funds, time, and interest.
Finds that fifth graders use both school and public libraries.

Type of literature:	Dissertation
Research method(s):	Questionnaire
Subject heading(s):	Libraries—Cooperation

079   *County and Regional Library Development* by Gretchen Knief
            Schenk. Chicago: American Library Association, 1954. 263p.
            LCCN 53-7488.
Addresses a then current void in the literature—a county and regional libraries manual. Identifies "the objectives of public library
service, i.e., education, information, aesthetic appreciation, research
and recreation," as not being different for municipal or large-unit
county libraries. Reports that the methods of obtaining these objectives are different in areas of special services, such as children's
services.

Also available with a 1972 publication date.

Type of literature:	Guidelines
Funding source(s):	American Library Association— Library Extension Division
Subject heading(s):	Libraries, Children's—Rural

080 "Creating the Library Habit" by Barbara Will Razzano. *Library Journal* 110:111–14 (Feb. 15, 1985).

Reports on a 1982 study of adult users in small public libraries of upstate New York, in terms of whether they visited the library as youngsters, how they visited the library (most with relatives), and why they used the library for the first time as children. Points out the importance of reference services to teenagers. Observes that parents who used the library as children ensure that their children use the library.

Type of literature:	Article—Research
Research method(s):	Questionnaire; Interviews
Subject heading(s):	Libraries, Children's—User Studies

081 "Crisis in the Southeast: Workshop Resolution." *West Virginia Libraries* 35:28–30 (Fall 1982).

Presents resolutions from the participants of the School and Children's Librarians Section of the Southeastern Library Association workshop held in June 1982 on intellectual freedom, library education, the Equal Rights Amendment, identification in Southern Association Standards, federal funding, and cooperative efforts.

Type of literature:	Policies
Subject heading(s):	Librarians, Children's— Education
	Libraries, Children's—Policies

082 "Current Trends in Public Library Service to Children," theme issue ed. by Winifred C. Ladley. *Library Trends* 12 (July 1983).

Identifies trends including services to handicapped children, introducing audiovisual materials into collections, and operating children's services within a "systems" organization. Discusses *Children's*

Service in Public Libraries and related research studies. See related entry for "The American Origins of Public Library Work with Children" (005).

Type of literature:	Article—Opinion
Subject heading(s):	Children—Handicapped
	Libraries, Children's—Services

083   "Dallas Public Library's Early Childhood Services" by Frances A. Smardo. *Top of the News* 40:207–13 (Winter 1984).
Reports on multicultural workshops for early childhood personnel, the research described in *What Research Tells Us about Storyhours and Receptive Language* (290), and the Art, Books and Child Care (ABC) Project for children in licensed child-care centers in Dallas. In the ABC Project, children created artwork based on quality literature that had been identified in bibliographies and at workshops.

Type of literature:	Article—Research
Funding source(s):	National Association for the Education of Young Children (NAEYC), Membership Action Grant (MAG)
	National Institute of Education, Office of Libraries and Learning Technologies
	Zale Corporation
Subject heading(s):	Children—Early Childhood
	Dallas Public Library
	Libraries, Children's—Programs and Activities

084   "The Development of Children's Book Reviewing in Selected Journals from 1924–1984" by Mary Ellen Meacham. Ph.D. Diss., Texas Woman's University, 1989. 187p. DAI 50/11A, p. 3400.
Examines *Booklist, Bulletin of the Center for Children's Books, Horn Book,* and *School Library Journal* in terms of style, quality, and length of reviews typical of each journal at different historical time periods. The journals' policies, number of reviewers, reviewers' backgrounds, and number of books reviewed were included in the study.

Type of literature:	Dissertation

Research method(s):   Reviews—Analysis
Subject heading(s):   Reviews and Reviewing

085 "Directory of National Youth-Serving Organizations" by
the Association for Library Service to Children (ALSC) and
Young Adult Services Division (YASD) liaison committees.
Top of the News 41:228–34 (Spring 1985).
Provides names, addresses, telephone numbers, contact persons,
missions, local chapters, publications, and conferences of organizations that serve youth.

Type of literature: Directory
Subject heading(s):   Organizations—Directories

086 "Early Appearances of Children's Reading Rooms in Public
Libraries" by Fannette H. Thomas. *Journal of Youth Services in
Libraries* 4:81–85 (Fall 1990).
Describes the physical facilities and decor of children's rooms in the
1890s.

Type of literature: Article—Historical
Subject heading(s):   Libraries, Children's—Facilities
                        Libraries, Children's—History—
                            United States

087 "Early Childhood Centers: Three Models" by Ellin Greene.
School Library Journal 30:21–27 (Feb. 1984).
Compares five centers: Media Library for Preschoolers, Erie Public Li-
brary, Erie, Pennsylvania; Preschool Adventure Library, Johnstown,
Pennsylvania; Center for Discovery, Columbus and Franklin County
Public Library, Columbus, Ohio; Gail Borden Public Library Chil-
dren's Center, Elgin, Illinois; and the Early Childhood Resource and
Information Center, New York Public Library, New York, New York.
Identifies necessary factors for success.

Type of literature: Article—Research
Research method(s):   Questionnaire; Site Visits
Subject heading(s):   Children—Early Childhood
                        Libraries, Children's—Programs
                            and Activities

088   *Early Childhood Creative Library, Interim Report* by Barbara
East. Elkin, N.C.: Northwestern Regional Library; Walnut
Cove, N.C.: Yadkin Valley Economic Development District,
Inc.; 1976. 48p. ED 124 206.
Identifies the objectives for, actions taken by, problems encountered
by, and corrections planned for this project, which trains parents
and baby sitters to teach preschool children by using educational
games and materials supplied by the library. Describes other aspects
of the project, including purchasing equipment for the community,
establishing story hours, providing transportation to the library, and
planning weekly library group activities.

Type of literature:	Report—Research
Funding source(s):	Bureau of Libraries and Learning Resources
Subject heading(s):	Children—Early Childhood Libraries, Children's—Programs and Activities

089   *Early Childhood Literature: Sharing Programs in Libraries* by
Ann D. Carlson. Hamden, Conn.: Library Professional Publications, 1985. ISBN 0-208-02068-3. ISSN 0-208-02074-8
(pbk). 119p.
Develops a scheme for linking the analysis of information about
child development from birth to three years of age with literature.
Examines practices and attitudes of librarians as they correspond to
the schema. Offers practical suggestions and identifies implications
for planning library experiences.
    Based on Carlson's dissertation, "Early Childhood Literature Shar-
ing Programs: Public Librarians' Practices and Attitudes." D.L.S.
Diss., Columbia University, 1983. 305p. DAI 46/08A, p. 2115.

Type of literature:	Book—Research
Research method(s):	Questionnaire
Subject heading(s):	Attitude Studies
	Children—Early Childhood
	Librarians, Children's
	Libraries, Children's—Programs and Activities

090 "Early Public Library Work with Children" by Shelley G. McNamara. *Top of the News* 43:59–72 (Fall 1986).
Describes libraries for children between 1876 and 1900 in terms of collections, facilities, and staffing. Identifies definitions of "children" and "library" as used by early writers.

Type of literature:	Article—Historical
Subject heading(s):	Libraries, Children's—History—United States

091 "Ebenezer Learned Had a Vision" by Alice M. Jordan. *Massachusetts Library Club Bulletin* 25:89–91 (Oct. 1935).
Contains quotes from Learned's last will, which is the earliest record of a specific bequest for a children's library. Highlights Learned's career and describes the establishment of the library, its collection, and its staff from 1835 to 1931.

Type of literature:	Article—Historical
Subject heading(s):	Learned, Ebenezer—Biographies
	Libraries, Children's—History—United States

092 "Educating Librarians to Serve Early Childhood" by Ellin Greene. *School Library Journal* 34:54 (Aug. 1988).
Describes coverage of materials and services to young children in the library education programs in the United States. Describes a course developed for the New York Public Library and offered at New York University.

Type of literature:	Article—Research
Funding source(s):	Carnegie Foundation
Research method(s):	Questionnaire
Subject heading(s):	Children—Early Childhood
	Librarians, Children's—Education

093 "Education of Librarians Working with Children in Public Libraries" by Sara Innis Fenwick. Master's Thesis, University of Chicago, 1951.

Identifies the objectives of library service to children, describes methods used by librarians to achieve those objectives, and identifies knowledge (other than library science) used by children's librarians. Examines the content of library school courses and makes recommendations.

Type of literature:	Master's Thesis
Research method(s):	Questionnaire
Subject heading(s):	Librarians, Children's—
	Competencies
	Librarians, Children's—
	Education

094   "The Educational Role and Services of Public Libraries in Indiana" by Shirley Fitzgibbons and Verna Pungitore. Bloomington, Ind.: School of Library and Information Science, 1988. 31p.
Documents the educational activities offered through Indiana's 239 public libraries. Identifies the provision of materials, reference, and information in support of parent education, preschool story time programs, visits to libraries by school classes, and other services.

Type of literature:	Report—Research
Funding source(s):	Indiana State Library
Research method(s):	Questionnaire
Subject heading(s):	Libraries, Children's—Services—
	Indiana

095   "The Effectiveness of Summer Reading Programs in Public Libraries in the United States" by Jill L. Locke. Ph.D. Diss., University of Pittsburgh, 1988. 186p. DAI 49/12A, p. 3539.
Examines the effectiveness of summer reading programs in reaching the total child population. Identifies factors related to success: the proportion of the child population compared to the total population, the age of children for whom the program was designed, marketing the program through school visits, a written evaluation report, the participation of the children's librarian in the design of the program, and the dissemination of the final evaluation report.

Type of literature:	Dissertation
Research method(s):	Questionnaire

Subject heading(s): Libraries, Children's—Programs
and Activities
Summer Reading Programs

096 "The Effects of a Storyhour and Book Borrowing Strategy on Emergent Reading Behavior in First-Grade Children" by Steven Lee Herb. Ph.D. Diss., Pennsylvania State University, 1987. 83p. DAI 48/04A, p. 886.
Finds that story hours with specially selected books, which the children take home for a week to read with their parents, positively affect the children's ability to read those texts. Recommends that children's librarians provide programming in the public school for children learning to read.

Type of literature: Dissertation
Research method(s): Experimental
Subject heading(s): Libraries, Children's—Programs
and Activities
Reading
Storyhours

097 "Effects of an English-only Law on Public Library Acquisition Policies, Practices, and Librarians' Attitudes toward Books in Spanish for Children and Young Adults" by Gene V. Glass and Isabel Schon. *Library and Information Science Research* 10:411–24 (Oct.-Dec. 1988).
Compares policies, practices, and attitudes after the passage of an English-only law with the results of an earlier study and finds no effect on policies and librarians' attitudes.

Type of literature: Article—Research
Research method(s): Interviews; Questionnaire
Subject heading(s): Attitude Studies
Libraries, Children's—Collections
Libraries, Children's—Materials—
Spanish

098 "Effects of Pre-School Programming upon Circulation of Children's Books in the Public Library" by Nancy R. Cummings. Master's Thesis, San Jose State University, 1976. 67p. ED 150 987.

Finds "a significant correlation between pre-school programming and the circulation of Easy books" (p. 49) and that parents attend the library and check out more materials when their children are attending programs. Describes and recommends the use of statistical and computer technology to gather accurate data and verification.

Type of literature:	Master's Thesis
Research method(s):	Questionnaire; Circulation Records—Analysis
Subject heading(s):	Libraries, Children's—Circulation Libraries, Children's—Programs and Activities

099   *Efficient Patterns for Adequate Library Service in a Large City: A Survey of Boston* by Leonard Grundt. University of Illinois, Graduate School of Library Science Monograph series, no. 6. Champaign-Urbana: University of Illinois, Graduate School of Library Science, 1968. 121p.

Hypothesizes that public library service outlets are not equally accessible to all residents of Boston. Assumes that the library should be within a half mile of the child's home, which is not the case. Concludes that branches tend to be children's libraries and the main library is oriented toward adult and young adult patrons.

Type of literature:	Report—Research
Research method(s):	Site Visits; Collection Analysis; Questionnaire
Subject heading(s):	Boston Public Library Libraries—Branches Libraries, Children's

100   *Eighty Years of Service: A History of the Children's Department, Seattle Public Library* by Linda J. Brass. Seattle, Wash.: Seattle Public Library, 1971. 65p.

Traces children's services at the Seattle Public Library from 1891 to 1971, including story hours, radio programs, television programs, services to schools, outreach programs, summer reading programs, monthly selection meetings, and many other creative programs. Documents the contributions of Gertrude Andrus, the first trained children's specialist. Speaks of the dedication of children's librarians, including those who, on a voluntary basis, told stories at the Japanese concentration camps.

Type of literature:	Report—Research
Subject heading(s):	Libraries, Children's—History—Seattle
	Seattle Public Library—History

101   *Emerging Library Systems: The 1963–66 Evaluation of the New York State Public Library Systems.* Albany: The University of the State of New York, State Education Department, Division of Evaluation, 1967. 291p.

Reports that "a great deal more enthusiasm, ingenuity, and imagination was demonstrated by local staff in handling the questions relating to materials for children than in handling those relating to adult resources" (p. 42). Notes that children account for 20 percent of the users of the public libraries and that accessibility is a problem for young children.

Type of literature:	Report—Research
Research method(s):	Annual Reports—Analysis; Interviews; Questionnaire; Site Visits
Subject heading(s):	Libraries, Children's—Services—New York State

102   *Evaluating Summer Reading Programs.* [Harrisburg]: Youth Services Division, Pennsylvania Library Association and the State Library of Pennsylvania, n.d. 20p.

Offers guidelines for planning a summer reading program, knowing the community, and establishing goals, objectives, and evaluation techniques for the program. Includes a sample survey for parents.

Type of literature:	Manual
Subject heading(s):	Libraries, Children's—Evaluation
	Summer Reading Programs

103   "Evaluating the Impact of Federally Funded Public Library Youth Programs" by Mary K. Chelton. In *Library Programs:*

Evaluating Federally Funded Public Library Programs, pp. 55–65, ed. by Betty Turok. Washington, D.C.: Superintendent of Documents, U.S. Government Printing Office, 1980.
Identifies the lack of operational client definitions, the lack of technical skill in evaluation, low organizational status, and absent documentation as key factors in hindering evaluation efforts. Offers steps to improve librarians' ability to evaluate through improved recognition and publicity, state or federally mandated service definitions, and subcontractor academic evaluators.

Type of literature:	Essay—Opinion
Subject heading(s):	Libraries, Children's—Evaluation

104   *Evaluation of the Children's Book Review Centers in Illinois* by Anne Billeter. Urbana: Library Research Center, University of Illinois, 1974. 66p. ED 102 527.
Determines that the centers did not improve the quality of selection. Recommends eliminating the centers not being used or lacking support from their library systems and strengthening the in-service programs at the others.

Type of literature:	Report—Research
Research method(s):	Questionnaire; Attendance Records Analysis
Subject heading(s):	Book Review Centers—Illinois

105   *Evaluation Report for Institute for Public Librarians in Service to Young Children, 1972–1973.* Durham: Learning Institute of North Carolina, 1973. 72p. ED 096 970.
Reports on the status of public library services for young children in North Carolina, the recruitment of librarians to specialize in early childhood library programs, and the expansion of the curriculum at North Carolina Central University's School of Library Science.

Type of literature:	Report—Institute
Funding source(s):	Higher Education Act, Title II-B
Subject heading(s):	Children—Preschoolers
	Librarians, Children's
	Libraries, Children's— Conferences and Institutes
	Libraries, Children's—Services— North Carolina

106   "Evaluation Report for Institute for Public Libraries in Service to Young Children" by Jeannie Price and Bernice Willis. Durham: School of Library Science, North Carolina Central University, 1972. 99p. ED 088 479.

Identifies the project goals as (1) to locate and describe public library services for young children in North Carolina, (2) to recruit public librarians who would benefit from the Early Childhood Specialist Library Program, and (3) to use the information and ideas gathered from the field and the students to expand the school's curriculum. Identifies competencies and educational needs of librarians serving young children.

Type of literature:	Report—Institute
Funding source(s):	Higher Education Act, Title II-B
Subject heading(s):	Children—Preschoolers
	Librarians, Children's
	Libraries, Children's—
	Conferences and Institutes
	Libraries, Children's—Services—
	North Carolina

107   "The Examination of Procedures and Practices in the Selection of Black Materials for Children's Collections of Public Libraries in the United States" by Emma Joyce White Mills. Ph.D. Diss., Florida State University, 1987. 227p. DAI 49/03A, p. 369.

Finds that selection of children's materials is influenced by reviews, children, parents, teachers, and library staff. Finds no significant differences between the short-term and long-term goals of public libraries for selecting more titles about minorities. Identifies the dominant group's members' pervasive attitude in their exclusion of materials based on their estimation of whether or not patrons will call for such materials.

Type of literature:	Dissertation
Research method(s):	Questionnaire; Selection
	Policies—Analysis
Subject heading(s):	Libraries, Children's—Collections
	Libraries, Children's—Policies
	Materials—Black

108   "An Exploratory Study of the Effect of a Public Library Summer Reading Club on Reading Skills" by Herbert Goldhor and John McCrossan. *Library Quarterly* 36:14–24 (Jan. 1966).
Tests "the hypothesis that children who join a public library summer reading club will receive significantly higher scores on a test of reading skill administered in the fall than children who do not join" (p. 18). Concludes that there is a relationship between the club membership and retention; however, previous reading ability has greater weight in predicting scores on reading tests.

Type of literature:	Article—Research
Funding source(s):	Illinois State Library
Subject heading(s):	Libraries, Children's—Programs and Activities
	Reading
	Summer Reading Programs

109   "First Analysis: Children's Services Survey" by Pat Behler. *Show Me Libraries* 33:15–17 (Dec. 1981).
Describes findings dealing with personnel, services, physical facilities, materials selection, budget, goals and objectives, and administrator's viewpoint. Project of the Children's Services Round Table of the Missouri Library Association in preparation for further statistical analysis and the development of standards for children's services in Missouri.

Type of literature:	Article—Research
Research method(s):	Questionnaire
Subject heading(s):	Libraries, Children's—Services— Missouri

110   *First Lessons: A Report on Elementary Education in America* by William J. Bennett. Washington, D.C.: U.S. Department of Education, 1986. 83p.
Explores the status of elementary schools, citing examples of successful practices and providing statistical data to enforce the importance of elementary education. As U.S. Secretary of Education, Bennett recommends that "every child should have and use a public library card" (p. 2).

Type of literature:	Report—Opinion
Subject heading(s):	Libraries, Children's

111 *Florida Long-Range Program for Library Service: An LSCA Five-Year Long-Range Plan.* Tallahassee, Fla.: Department of State, Division of Library and Information Services, 1989. Consists of 22 sections, each independently paged.

Identifies in section 16 the long-range objectives and immediate objectives relating to library service to youth, covering staffing, collections, services, cooperation with other agencies, accessibility, and in-service programs.

Type of literature:	Report—Planning
Funding source(s):	Library Services and Construction Act
Subject heading(s):	Libraries, Children's—Florida

112 *Foundations of Quality: Guidelines for Public Library Service to Children.* Cover title: *Guidelines for Public Library Service to Children.* Chicago: Illinois Library Association, Children's Librarians' Section, 1981. 14p.

Offers guidelines for public library services to children in terms of goals, evaluation, budget, personnel, services, programs, materials, equipment, and facilities. Appendix includes ALA's "Library Bill of Rights."

Working version available in "Foundations of Quality: Guidelines for Public Library Service to Children" by Susan Roman. *Illinois Libraries* 62:923–29 (Dec. 1980).

Type of literature:	Guidelines
Subject heading(s):	Libraries, Children's—Guidelines—Illinois

113 *The Free Library and the Revitalization of Philadelphia: A Program for the 1980's* by Lowell A. Martin, Faith McDowell, and Nancy Magnuson. Philadelphia: Free Library of Philadelphia, 1981.

Identifies the functions being carried out by the library and recommends that for the 1980s five focal points be emphasized in setting priorities. One recommendation was for branch libraries to serve as reading and media centers. Observes that although children's use has been on the decline, the number of children registered represents 43 percent of the population, while adults represent 28 percent. More specific recommendations address services, staffing, activities, audiovisual materials, needs of preschoolers, work with teachers, and range of book collections.

Type of literature:	Report—Research
Subject heading(s):	Libraries, Children's—
	Administration and
	Organization
	Libraries, Children's—
	Philadelphia
	Philadelphia, Free Library of

114   "From Idealism to Realism: Library Directors and Children's Services" by Dorothy J. Anderson. *Library Trends* 35:393–412 (Winter 1987).

Traces the attitudes of library directors toward children's services since the 1800s, noting the renewed interest in children and youth in the 1980s. Directors reported the need for in-service programs to attract children as library users so they will become adult users and library supporters.

Type of literature:	Article—Research
Research method(s):	Interviews
Subject heading(s):	Librarians, Children's
	Libraries, Children's

115   "From Superstition to Science: The Role of Research in Strengthening Public Library Service to Children" by M. Leslie Edmonds. *Library Trends* 35:509–20 (Winter 1987).

Notes the call for systematic research since the 1940s. Highlights research in the areas of reading, school and public library cooperation, as well as measurement and accountability. Describes factors needed to create a favorable research climate, including attitudes, support, technical design, children as subjects, implementation of research, and recruitment of doctoral students.

Type of literature:	Article—Opinion
Subject heading(s):	Librarians, Children's—
	Education
	Libraries, Children's—Research

116 "The Frontiers of Library Service for Youth" by Frances Henne. In *Youth, Communication, and Libraries*, pp. 209–22, ed. by Frances Henne, Alice Brooks, and Ruth Ersted. Chicago: American Library Association, 1949.

Discusses ten goals for library service: (1) achieving equality of opportunity, (2) implementing standards, (3) developing interpretive services, (4) serving as materials specialist, (5) freeing librarians from technical processes, (6) working with other agencies, (7) establishing regional or national materials examination centers, (8) strengthening national, state, and regional planning, (9) recruiting, and (10) developing a systematic program of research.

Type of literature: Essay—Opinion
Subject heading(s):   Librarians, Children's
    Libraries, Children's—Goals and Objectives

117 "The Future of Library Work with Children: A Symposium." *Library Journal* 61:817–20 (Nov. 1, 1936), 919–23 (Dec. 1, 1936), 17–21 (Jan. 1, 1937), 14–15 (Feb. 1, 1937).

Includes the following essays: (1) Louise P. Latimer on the need for well-educated and experienced children's librarians, (2) Carrie E. Scott on the expansion of formats and outreach services, (3) Annie I. M. Jackson on training children to be adult users, (4) Clarence E. Sherman on maintaining and improving services, (5) Alice I. Haseltine on the need for research and methods of measurement, (6) Siri M. Andrews on education and competencies, (7) Effie L. Power on cooperation of professional organizations and education of public library administrators, (8) Lillian H. Smith on the importance of quality literature, and (9) Gladys English on the need for children's librarians to become more active in regional and state developments.

Type of literature: Article—Opinion
Subject heading(s):   Librarians, Children's
    Libraries, Children's—Goals and Objectives

118 "The Genesis of Children's Services in the American Public Library: 1875–1906" by Fannette Henrietta Thomas. Ph.D. Diss., University of Wisconsin-Madison, 1982. 376p. DAI 43/10A, p. 3147.

Traces the factors influencing the evolution of children's services through study of the Boston Public Library, Brookline Public Library, Carnegie Library of Pittsburgh, Cleveland Public Library, Denver Public Library, Hartford Public Library, Pawtucket Public Library, Pratt Institute of Brooklyn, Providence Public Library, and Worcester Public Library.

Type of literature:	Dissertation
Research method(s):	Historical
Subject heading(s):	Boston Public Library—History
	Brookline Public Library—History
	Brooklyn, Pratt Institute of—History
	Cleveland Public Library—History
	Denver Public Library—History
	Hartford Public Library—History
	Libraries, Children's—History
	Milwaukee Public Library—History
	New York Public Library—History
	Pawtucket Public Library—History
	Pittsburgh, Carnegie Library of—History
	Providence Public Library—History
	Worcester Public Library—History

119   "Goals for Children's Services in Public Libraries" by Mary E. Kingsbury. *School Library Journal* 24:19–21 (Jan. 1978).

Discusses a modified Delphi study and identifies eleven goals rated highest priority by at least 50 percent of the responding children's librarians and coordinators. The first three goals are (1) making coordinators a part of the planning team, (2) recognizing the rights of all children to library services and materials, and (3) providing the widest possible selection of materials.

Type of literature:	Article—Research
Research method(s):	Delphi

Subject heading(s): Libraries, Children's—Goals and
     Objectives
     Libraries, Children's—Services

120 *The Good Seed: Library Planning for Urban Disadvantaged Children Ages Three to Seven* by Eleanor R. McKinney and Valerie Noble. Kalamazoo: Department of Librarianship, Western Michigan University, 1970. 30p.
Describes characteristics of disadvantaged children, elements of a successful program to meet their needs, and recommended materials. Reports on a two-week institute attended by teams of children's librarians and school librarians from the same community.
  Type of literature: Report—Institute
  Funding source(s): U.S. Office of Education, Department of Health, Education and Welfare
  Subject heading(s): Children—Disadvantaged
        Libraries, Children's—
         Conferences and Institutes
        Libraries, Children's—Services

121 *Guide to Children's Libraries and Literature outside the United States*, compiled by Amy Kellman. Chicago: American Library Association, 1982. 32p. ISBN 0-8389-3254-1 (pbk).
Identifies institutions and organizations in the United States that supply information about libraries for children, research collections of children's literature, and children's book publishing in other countries. Lists selected books, periodical articles, and other publications with background information about children's literature abroad. Arranged geographically by continent, then country.
  Type of literature: Directory
  Subject heading(s): Libraries, Children's—United States

122 *Guidelines for Children's Services* by Ann Gagnon. Library Service to Children series, no. 1. [Ottawa]: Canadian Library Association, 1989. 20p. ISBN 0-88802-221-2.

Offers suggestions for providing library services to children in terms
of administration, facilities, services, access, staffing, and public relations. Includes sample goals and objectives. Other titles in the series
provide more information on these topics.

      Type of literature: Guidelines
      Subject heading(s):   Libraries, Children's—
                                Guidelines—Canada

123   *Guidelines for Children's Services in Public Libraries of New Jer-*
       sey. Trenton: New Jersey State Library, New Jersey State De-
       partment of Education, 1987. 66p.
Describes each of four components: services, resources, facilities, and
staffing and operations. Identifies goals and provides a checklist of
considerations to use in the planning process. Appendixes include
the "Library Bill of Rights" and the "Freedom to Read."
    Available for purchase for $6. Make check payable to Treasurer,
State of New Jersey. Send request to GUIDELINES, Library Development Bureau, New Jersey State Library, 185 W. State St., CN 520,
Trenton, NJ 08625-0520.

      Type of literature: Guidelines
      Subject heading(s):   Libraries, Children's—
                                Guidelines—New Jersey
                                Libraries, Children's—Goals and
                                Objectives
                                Libraries, Children's—Planning

124   *Guidelines for Public Library Service to Children in Vermont*
       by the Vermont Department of Libraries, Task Force on
       Children's Services. Montpelier: Vermont Department of Li-
       braries, 1988. 24p.
Presents a philosophy of library service to children and offers guide-
lines for staffing, materials, programming, facilities, and the role of
trustees. Appendixes include the "Library Bill of Rights" and "Free
Access to Libraries for Minors."
    Available for $5 from the Vermont Department of Libraries, 109
State St., Pavilion Office Building, Montpelier, VT 05602.

      Type of literature: Guidelines

Subject heading(s):   Libraries, Children's—
                          Guidelines—Vermont
                          Libraries, Children's—Philosophy

125   *Guidelines for Young People's Library Service in Nebraska.* Lin-
          coln: Nebraska State Library, n.d. Photocopied. 4p.
Offers guidelines in terms of children's rights and accessibility, staff,
administration, budget, physical facilities, materials and programming, as well as state and system commitment to young people's
services.
          Type of literature: Guidelines
          Subject heading(s):   Libraries, Children's—
                                    Guidelines—Nebraska

126   "Happy Birthday, TON!: A Brief Look at Its First Forty Years"
          by Carolyn Baggett. *Top of the News* 39:114–17 (Fall 1982).
Traces the journal from its first appearance in 1942 as an eight-page
quarterly house organ and news bulletin, noting the first photo-
graph in 1946 and the introduction of advertising in 1947, and high-
lighting the topics covered through the years. TON is the forerunner
of *Journal of Youth Services in Libraries.*
          Type of literature: Article—Historical
          Subject heading(s):   Association for Library Service to
                                    Children—Periodicals
                                    Top of the News—History

127   *A Head Start at the Library.* "Check This Out" series. Washing-
          ton, D.C.: Office of Libraries and Learning Technologies,
          1989. 4p. ED 317 210.
Describes a program designed to provide Head Start children with
opportunities to obtain a Denver Public Library card and to visit
the library. Also features programs for Head Start staff, public library
personnel, and the families of Head Start children.
          Type of literature: Report—Demonstration Project
          Funding source(s):   Library Services and Construction
                                    Act
          Subject heading(s):   Children—Head Start
                                    Libraries, Children's—Services

51

128 "A History and Analysis of *Top of the News*, 1942–1987" by Marilyn H. Karrenbrock. *Journal of Youth Services in Libraries* 1:29–43 (Fall 1987).

Traces the history of the journal and discusses feature items: types; length; authors; subjects; age levels; and service sites. Identifies trends in the journal.

Type of literature:	Article—Research
Research method(s):	Content Analysis
Subject heading(s):	Association for Library Service to Children—Periodicals
	Top of the News—History

129 "The History and Development of Hawaii Public Libraries: The Library of Hawaii and Hawaii State Library: 1913–1971" by Chieko Tachihata. Ph.D. Diss., University of Southern California, 1981. 373p. DAI 41/06A, p. 2345.

Traces the development of the Library of Hawaii and county libraries to the formation of the Hawaii State Library System, beginning with statehood, when the Central Library became the Hawaii State Library and the central metropolitan library for Honolulu. Reports that the American influence and westernization of the Asian population affected the role of the public library, particularly in the area of children's services. Notes that in 1913 the children's room began its patterns of services to children, parents, and schools, but by the late 1950s there was a nationwide shortage of children's librarians.

Type of literature:	Dissertation
Research method(s):	Historical
Subject heading(s):	Hawaii State Library—History
	Libraries, Children's—History—Hawaii

130 *History of Libraries in the Western World* by Elmer D. Johnson. 2nd ed. Metuchen, N.J.: Scarecrow Press, 1970. 521p. ISBN 0-8108-0183-X.

Includes library services to youth in the United States from 1790 to 1960 and briefly mentions children's services in Canada.

Type of literature:	Book—Historical
Subject heading(s):	Libraries, Children's—History

131   "A History of the Children's Department of the Free Library of Philadelphia, 1898–1953" by Barbara Hayes Ambler. Master's Thesis, Drexel Institute of Technology, 1956. 72p.
Reveals a period of growth and activity followed by one of shortages and curtailment due to lack of funds in the 1930s. Describes reorganization and enlargement in the 1950s. Identifies continuing policies that have affected the program: (1) support from the library's administrators and (2) cooperation with local agencies. Traces the fifty-year history of the story hour program from 1903 and the thirty-year history of the vacation reading program.

Type of literature:	Master's Thesis
Research method(s):	Historical
Subject heading(s):	Libraries, Children's—History
	Philadelphia, Free Library of— History

132   "Hopes and Expectations of Children's Librarians" by Adele Fasick. *Canadian Library Journal* 37:331–33 (Oct. 1980).
Reports what children's librarians think about the need to develop management skills, including their discouragement about having less chance than other librarians to be promoted to administrative jobs; their responses when told that they need adult library experience to be branch librarians, but that adult librarians do not need experience with youth; and the difference between librarians with library school education and those without, in terms of desired workshops and courses. Concludes that professional associations and library schools should address these needs. Calls for librarians to let schools know what they need and want.

Type of literature:	Article—Research
Research method(s):	Questionnaire
Subject heading(s):	Librarians, Children's—Career Goals
	Librarians, Children's— Education

133   "An Image/Status Study" by Alice Calabrese. *Illinois Libraries* 58:792–94 (Dec. 1976).
Examines children's librarians' perceptions of having lower status than other librarians. Reports that those who were consulted about

library policy matters had feelings of increased status; others noted lower salaries, not being consulted, and that the perception of others about the less demanding responsibilities of children's librarians caused a lower perception of status.

Type of literature:	Article—Research
Research method(s):	Questionnaire
Subject heading(s):	Librarians, Children's

134   "Images of Librarians and Librarianship: A Study" by Joan R. Duffy. *Journal of Youth Services in Libraries* 3:303–8 (Summer 1990).

Reports on interviews with young people, ages four to fifteen, regarding their career goals and whether they would want to be a librarian. Includes misconceptions of what librarians do. Identifies librarians' helpfulness as their most favored quality. Describes the drawings of librarians by the interview participants.

Type of literature:	Article—Research
Research method(s):	Interviews; Children's
	Drawings—Analysis
Subject heading(s):	Librarians, Children's

135   "Implementation: Using Foundations of Quality to Underpin Avenues to Excellence" by Susan Roman. *Illinois Libraries* 67:2–4 (Jan. 1985).

Surveys fifth to eighth graders to determine their reading interests, library use, and how they learned about titles they wanted to read. Uses volunteers as reviewers and publishes their efforts on a quarterly basis. Conducts interviews with the reviewers six years later to evaluate their experiences.

Type of literature:	Article—Research
Research method(s):	Questionnaire; Interviews
Subject heading(s):	Reviews and Reviewing

136   "The Importance of Every Child Using and Obtaining a Public Library Card." *Top of the News* 43:237–38 (Spring 1987).

Responding to William J. Bennett's belief that every child should have a library card (see *First Lessons: A Report on Elementary Education in America* [110]), the American Library Association Council passed this resolution calling for the American Library Association and the

Association for Library Service to Children to initiate a campaign in cooperation with the nation's schools to ensure that every child obtained and used a public library card by the end of the 1987–88 school year.

    Type of literature: Policies
    Subject heading(s):   Libraries, Children's—Policies

137   "Improving Children's Services: Competencies for Librarians Serving Children in Public Libraries" by Barbara Immroth. *Public Libraries* 28:166–69 (May-June 1989).

Traces the development of competency statements for school librarians, young adult librarians, and children's librarians. Offers recommendations for the use of the Association for Library Service to Children's "Competencies for Librarians Serving Children in Public Libraries" by library educators, public library administrators, state and regional agencies, librarians, library school students, and professional associations. The ALSC statement is printed in full.

    Type of literature: Article—Opinion
    Subject heading(s):   Librarians, Children's—
                          Competencies
                          Libraries, Children's—Staffing

138   "In Search of . . . Standards for Youth Services in the Pioneer Library System of New York State" by Linda Clark Benedict. *Bookmark* 24:176–77 (Spring 1988).

Reports how libraries within the system were meeting the 1984 New York Library Association's *Standards for Youth Services in Public Libraries of New York*. Finds that (1) fewer than 60 percent of the respondents had a written selection policy, (2) reference services including interlibrary loan were available to youth, and (3) libraries exceeded the recommended number of programs, but were weaker in their use of technology and budgets for children's materials.

    Type of literature: Article—Research
    Research method(s):   Questionnaire
    Subject heading(s):   Libraries, Children's—New York
                          State

139   "Information Services in Central Children's Libraries" by Mae E. Benne. *School Library Journal* 26:25 (April 1980).

Focuses on the information and reference services section of Benne's fuller report, *The Central Children's Library in Metropolitan Public Libraries*, noting the use of the central children's libraries by scholars studying children's literature, adults seeking information, and children. The children had access to adult collections and reserves, although there were some cases of limitations on the children's use. Twenty-seven central children's libraries had total or partial responsibility for historical materials. Other materials offered included reference works about children's literature, information on community organizations, and special subject indexes. Various patterns of providing bibliographic access were found, including the lack of full bibliographic access in the main catalog.

Type of literature: Article—Research
Research method(s):   Site Visits
Subject heading(s):   Libraries, Children's—Central
                             Library
                             Libraries, Children's—
                             Metropolitan
                             Libraries, Children's—Reference
                             Services

140   "Innovations in Children's Services in Public Libraries" by
            Mary E. Kingsbury. *Top of the News* 35:39–42 (Fall 1978).
Identifies ten innovations prioritized by coordinators of children's services in the fifty largest cities in the United States. Changes included are: making library directors aware that children's librarians have the potential to provide leadership for the entire library; hiring active, energetic children's librarians; increasing collections of high-interest, low-vocabulary materials; increasing outreach services; establishing information retrieval systems; and providing separate auditoriums for children's services with stage equipment, as well as an activity room and a quiet room.

Type of literature: Article—Research
Research method(s):   Questionnaire
Subject heading(s):   Libraries, Children's—Services

141   *Inspection of Library Training Schools, 1914: The Missing Robbins Report* by Charles A. Seavey. Occasional Papers no.186.

Champaign-Urbana: Graduate School of Library and Information Science, University of Illinois, 1989. 67p. ISSN 0276-1769.

Includes a description of the "Training School for Children's Librarians of the Carnegie Library of Pittsburgh" in terms of courses offered, relation to other institutions, housing and equipment, instructors, requirements for admission, attention given to students outside school hours, curriculum, graduates, and positions. The description concludes: "A fine example of a special course well-planned and carried out. The harmony between instructors and students is very marked" (p. 50).

Reprint of the "Inspection of Library Training Schools, 1914: Report to the ALA Committee on Library Training" by Mary Esther Robbins.

Type of literature:	Report—Evaluation
Subject heading(s):	Librarians, Children's—Education

142   "Interim Guidelines for Public Library Service to Children in California" by the Children's Services Standards Committee. [Sacramento]: California Library Association, 1980. Unp.

Identifies qualitative guidelines for service, collection development (selection, budgeting), physical facilities, personnel, and administration.

Type of literature:	Standards
Subject heading(s):	Libraries, Children's—Standards—California

143   *The Introduction to Children's Work in Public Libraries* by Dorothy M. Broderick. New York: H. W. Wilson, 1965. 176p. LCCN 64-22813.

Addressing the needs of librarians who are responsible for providing service for all age groups within a community, the author presents a philosophy of service to children, identifies the problems of book selection, covers the operation of a children's room, and discusses programming and community relations. Taking the position that the first job is to build a collection and the second is to get it used, the author discusses different types of children's books.

Type of literature:	Book—Opinion

Subject heading(s):   Libraries, Children's

144 *An Inventory of Library Services and Resources of the State of Washington 1965* by L. Dorothy Bevis. Olympia: Washington State Library, 1968. 385p.

Uses the 1956 standards *Public Library Service: A Guide to Evaluation with Minimum Standards* to assess the libraries. Arranged by population served. The descriptions for children's services cover analysis of collections, programming, summer reading programs, and class visits. Reports on a library serving fewer than 5,000 patrons that required children to be accompanied by an adult.

        Type of literature: Report—Research
        Research method(s):   Questionnaires
        Subject heading(s):   Libraries, Children's—Statistics—
                                    Washington

145 "An Investigation of Existing Approaches to the Problem of Providing Library Service in the Rural Kansas Community: A Study of the Interrelationships of the Public Library and the Public School Library in Selected Rural Communities of Kansas" by Allen R. Grunau. Ed.D. Diss., University of Kansas, 1965. 212p. DAI 27/01A, p. 219.

Observes that schools have accreditation standards and are the only libraries in some communities. Points out that the successful patterns of cooperation reflect the unique needs and resources of each community. Concludes that "where possible, separate but cooperating library units are desirable" (p. 169).

        Type of literature: Dissertation
        Major professor: William York
        Research method(s):   Site Visits; Case Studies;
                                    Questionnaire
        Subject heading(s):   Libraries—Rural—Kansas
                                    School and Public Libraries—
                                    Kansas

146 *An Investigation of the Effectiveness of an Online Catalog in Providing Bibliographic Access to Children in a Public Library Setting. Research Report* by Leslie Edmonds, Paula Moore, and Kathleen Mehaffey Balcom. Champaign-Urbana: Graduate

School of Library and Information Science, University of Illinois, 1989. 98p. ED 311-921.

Evaluates the use of an online catalog by children in comparison with their use of a card catalog. Reports on the testing of thirty-three children (fourth, sixth, and eighth grades) to determine whether they had the developmental skills needed to locate and interpret bibliographic information presented in both forms of the catalog. Reports that the children did not have a broad knowledge of alphabetizing or filing conventions and were able to successfully complete 65 percent of the card catalog searches and only 18 percent of the online searches. Calls for the development of software using natural language, fewer screens, and clearer help messages, and for library instruction to help children develop the necessary skills.

Type of literature:	Report—Research
Research method(s):	Observation; Interviews
Subject heading(s):	Libraries, Children's—Cataloging
	Libraries, Children's—User
	Studies

147   "Invisible Women: The Children's Librarian in America" by Margo Sasse. *School Library Journal* 19:21–25 (Jan. 1973).

Highlights the early development of children's services, focusing on the contributions of pioneers (Minera Amanda Sanders and Anne Carroll Moore). Notes the lack of attention given to the early leaders of children's services in the *Dictionary of American Biography, National Cyclopedia of American Biography* and *Notable American Women, 1607–1950.*

Type of literature:	Article—Historical
Subject heading(s):	Librarians, Children's
	Librarians, Children's—
	Biographies

148   "Jobs Gone Begging: Personnel Needs and Youth Services" by Richard Ashford. *School Library Journal* 31:19–24 (Nov. 1984).

Examines personnel vacancies in New England to document the options open to students. Reports that for entry-level positions, catalogers and children's librarians are consistently high in terms of

need. Observes that salary levels for youth services positions discour-
age graduates who compare those salaries with those of special libraries positions. Calculates that when one looks at average salaries,
the person should choose a position based on personal inclination
rather than a position rumored to pay well. Calls for library schools
to recruit in the youth services area and for employers to encourage
staff members to consider library school.

> Type of literature: Article—Research
> Research method(s):   Job Announcements—Analysis
> Subject heading(s):   Librarians, Children's—Job
>   Announcements

149 *Journal of Youth Services in Libraries.* Quarterly. 50 E. Huron
        St., Chicago, IL 60611.
This journal of the Association for Library Service to Children and
the Young Adult Library Services Association of the American Library
Association was formerly titled *Top of the News*. A regular feature is
the "Focus on Research" column.

> Type of literature: Journal
> Subject heading(s):   Association for Library Service to
>   Children—Periodicals
>   Libraries, Children's—Periodicals

150 "Keeping Out of Trouble: Research and Children's Services
        of Public Libraries" by Mary E. Kingsbury. In *Children's Ser-
        vices in Public Libraries*, pp. 131–47, ed. by Selma K. Richard-
        son. Urbana-Champaign: Graduate School of Library Sci-
        ence, University of Illinois, 1978.
Reviews methodologies commonly used in research and proposes
an ethnographic study of a children's librarian. Suggests that Mae
Benne's *The Central Children's Library in Metropolitan Public Libraries*
(031) "may well become a landmark study in the history of children's
services in public libraries" (p. 138). Offers suggestions for further
research and discusses the problems of where to publish research
findings. Describes Pauline Wilson's "Barriers to Research in Library
Schools: A Framework for Analysis."

> Type of literature: Article—Opinion
> Subject heading(s):   Librarians, Children's—Research
>   Libraries, Children's—Research

151 "Kid Stuff: A Policy That Works for Two Cities" by William Mueller. *Library Journal* 112:48–51 (March 1, 1987).
Describes the development and implementation of the Iowa City Public Library's "Library Policy on Unwanted Children and/or Disruptive Behavior" by the library and by the Cedar Rapids Libraries. Addresses children left unattended and disruptive behavior by children younger than age nine, whether or not attended by an adult, and by children older than age nine.

Type of literature:	Policy
Subject heading(s):	Libraries, Children's—Policies

152 "Kids Are Rural, Too!" by Marlys Cresap. *Rural Library Service Newsletter* 1–4 (Aug. 1986).
Reports on a conference entitled "Library Service to Rural Children" held March 21–22, 1986, under the sponsorship of the Iowa State Library. Highlights speeches by Margaret Bush (trends in children's services and models for children's services), Marilyn Nickelsbury (survey of strengths and weaknesses of children's service in rural libraries in Iowa), and Barbara Will Razzano (role of children's librarians). Describes the activities of the participants (writing a philosophy statement, analyzing case studies).

Type of literature:	Report—Conference
Research method(s):	Questionnaire
Subject heading(s):	Libraries, Children's—Conferences and Institutes
	Libraries, Children's—Rural—Iowa
	Libraries, Children's—Services—Iowa

153 "Kids Need Libraries: School and Public Libraries Preparing the Youth of Today for the World of Tomorrow" by Virginia H. Mathews, Judith G. Flum, and Karen A. Whitney. *Journal of Youth Services in Libraries* 3:197–207 (Spring 1990).
Addresses the themes of the Second White House Conference on Library and Information Services on behalf of the three youth services divisions of the American Library Association (American Association of School Librarians, Association for Library Service to Children, and Young Adult Services Division). Provides a state and local checklist

for assessing how libraries can serve youth and offers recommendations for action at the conference.

Also available in *School Library Media Quarterly* 18:167–72 (Spring
1990).

        Type of literature: Policy
        Subject heading(s):   Libraries, Children's
                               White House Conference on Li-
                                 brary and Information Services,
                               Second

154   *Kids Welcome Here! Writing Public Library Policies That Promote
       Use by Young People,* ed. by Anne E. Simon. Albany: New
       York Library Association, Youth Services Section, 1990. 128p.
       ISSN 0-9316-5828-4.

Covers philosophy, communications, library trustees, access to library services, collection development, reference services, programming policies, and library conduct.

Copies available for $13 each from the New York Library Associ-
ation, 252 Hudson Ave., Albany, NY 12210-1802.

        Type of literature: Manual
        Subject heading(s):   Libraries, Children's—Policies

155   *Lands of Pleasure: Essays on Lillian H. Smith and the Develop-
       ment of Children's Libraries,* ed. by Adele M. Fasick, Margaret
       M. Johnston, and Ruth Osler. Metuchen, N.J.: Scarecrow
       Press, 1990. 176p. ISBN 0-81-8-2266-0. LCCN 89-70024.*

Describes Lillian H. Smith's influence on the development of children's libraries in Canada, the United States, and the world. Includes
a bibliography of her writings.

See also "Carrying on the Tradition: Training Librarians for Children's Services" (030).

        Type of literature: Book—Opinion
        Subject heading(s):   Librarians, Children's—
                                 Biographies
                               Libraries, Children's—Canada
                               Libraries, Children's—United
                               States
                               Smith, Lillian Helena—
                               Biographies

156 *Latchkey Children in the Public Library: Resources for Planners* by the Service to Children Committee, Public Library Association, a division of the American Library Association, in collaboration with the Library Service to Children with Special Needs Committee of the Association for Library Service to Children, a division of the American Library Association. Chicago: American Library Association, 1988. 76p.

Presents a model policy development process, recommends programs, and makes suggestions to spare public libraries the problem of unsupervised children. Appendixes include bibliographies for librarians and for children, a list of libraries having policies, and a legal opinion covering the library's duty to supervise unattended children and the library's liability for such children.

Type of literature:	Policies
Subject heading(s):	Children—Latchkey
	Libraries, Children's—Policies
	and Procedures

157 "Librarians' Satisfaction with the Subject Access to Children's Materials Provided by Library Catalogs" by Kathleen Margaret Tessmer. Ph.D. Diss., University of Wisconsin–Madison, 1984. 262p. DAI 45/12A, p. 3471.

Analyzes and compares the responses of Wisconsin children's librarians, school librarians, and catalogers regarding the adequacy of subject access, areas most and least satisfactory, and library practices associated with their satisfaction or dissatisfaction. Reports that both school and public library respondents were unaware of the ALA's Resources and Technical Services Division/Cataloging and Classification Section (CCS) guidelines recommending that Library of Congress subject headings augmented by special children's subject headings be used as the standard for cataloging children's materials.

Type of literature:	Dissertation
Major professor:	Mary S. Woodworth
Research method(s):	Questionnaire
Subject heading(s):	Libraries, Children's—Cataloging

158 *Libraries Improve Florida's Education: A Report on the Role of Public Libraries in the Education of Florida's Children and Illiterate Adults* by E. Walter Terrie and F. William Summers.

Tallahassee: Florida Department of State, Division of Library
and Information Services, 1987. 31p. LCCN 87-622997.
Reports that "at least half of the work done by public libraries with
young people is for an educational purpose" (p. 5). Identifies fifteen
types of services for youth, including infant and toddler programs,
preschool programs, parent education, class visits to the library, librarian visits to schools, workshops for teachers and day-care work-
ers, summer reading programs, and classroom collection loans.

Type of literature:	Report—Research
Funding source(s):	Library Services and Construction Act
Research method(s):	Questionnaire
Subject heading(s):	Libraries, Children's—Services— Florida

159   *Library Cooperation: The Brown University Study of University-
School-Community Library Coordination in the State of Rhode
Island* by John A. Humphry. Providence, R.I.: Brown University Press, 1963. 213p. LCCN 62-21919.
Addresses ways to achieve more effective coordination of library
service. Describes deteriorating collections, inadequate library services to children, and the lack of suitable facilities. Recommends
improvements (staffing, collections, and facilities) and the use of
library councils.

Type of literature:	Report—Research
Funding source(s):	Council on Library Resources
Research method(s):	Site Visits
Subject heading(s):	Libraries, Children's—Services— Rhode Island
	Libraries—Cooperation
	School and Public Libraries

160   "Library Education and Youth Services: A Survey of Faculty
Course Offerings, and Related Activities in Accredited Library Schools" by Melody Lloyd Allen and Margaret Bush.
Library Trends 25:485–508 (Winter 1987).
Describes youth services (children's, young adult's, and school) offerings in terms of library school courses (number of offerings, topics, enrollment), courses outside the library school, specialization

beyond the M.L.S., faculty (interests, projects), and continuing education offerings. Concludes that there are opportunities for students to specialize in youth services.

Highlights of this survey appear in "Professional Education for Youth Services Librarians: A Preliminary Report" by Melody Lloyd Allen and Margaret A. Bush. *Top of the News* 42:423–25 (Summer 1986).

Type of literature:	Article—Research
Funding source(s):	Emily Hollowell Research Fund, Simmons College
Research method(s):	Questionnaire
Subject heading(s):	Librarians, Children's— Education

161 *Library Service for Children* by Effie L. Power. Chicago: American Library Association, 1930. 320p. LCCN 30-32561.

Traces the development of children's libraries and the values on which they were based. Addresses the role of the librarian, offering suggestions for research studies. Identifies research projects and questions at the end of each chapter. Describes the educational preparation children's librarians need. Emphasizes the library as a place for children to read. Cited by other writers as the authoritative work for this period.

Type of literature:	Book—Opinion
Subject heading(s):	Libraries, Children's—Goals and Objectives
	Libraries, Children's—Research
	Libraries, Children's—Services

162 *Library Service in Pennsylvania: Present and Proposed* by Lowell A. Martin. Harrisburg: Pennslyvania State Library, 1958. 177p. LCCN 59-9611.

Describes a survey of public, college, and special libraries, in which it was found that 11.7 percent of the libraries had children's librarians and 34.7 percent offered story hours. Recommends that children have a library within one mile of their homes. Calls for demonstration libraries, increased staff at the State Library to handle in-service programs, and statewide coordination of library education.

Type of literature:	Report—Research

Funding source(s):   Pennsylvania State Library
Research method(s):   Interviews; Questionnaire; Case
                            Studies; Site Visits
Subject heading(s):   Libraries, Children's—Services—
                            Pennsylvania
                            Libraries, State—Pennsylvania

163   "Library Service to Children—A Job or a Profession?" by Diana Young. *Public Libraries* 24:24–26 (Spring 1981).
Describes the competencies and commitment needed by children's librarians and lists the goals established in 1973 by the Task Force on Children's Services of the Public Library Association.
Type of literature: Article—Opinion
Subject heading(s):   Librarians, Children's—
                            Competencies
                            Libraries, Children's—Goals and
                            Objectives

164   "Library Services and Construction Act, FFY 1991–1995, Long Range Program" by the Oklahoma Department of Libraries. Oklahoma City: Oklahoma Department of Libraries, 1990. 199p.
Identifies objectives for improving library service to children through an increase in the juvenile circulation per capita level, an increase in the number of children's programs offered, and an increase in trained children's staff persons. Includes statistics about circulation, programming, and staffing for 1989.
Type of literature: Report—Planning
Subject heading(s):   Libraries, Children's—Planning—
                            Oklahoma
                            Libraries, Children's—Statistics—
                            Oklahoma

165   *Library Services for Hispanic Children: A Guide for Public and School Librarians* by Adela Artola Allen. Phoenix, Ariz.: Oryx Press, 1987. 201p. ISBN 0-89774-371-7. LCCN 86-42799.
Traces the history of services to Hispanic children and describes the approaches used. Identifies professional issues, including Hispanic

culture, the management of library programs and services, guide-lines for selecting and acquiring materials, classification and cata-loging concerns, strategies for involving children in reading, the lan-guage of literature, etymology, and English-Spanish library-related vocabulary. Recommends materials and their sources.

Type of literature:	Book—Opinion
Subject heading(s):	Children—Hispanic
	Libraries, Children's—Materials—
	Spanish
	Libraries, Children's—Services

166 "Library Standards for Juvenile Correctional Institutions" by the American Correctional Association/ALA Health and Re-habilitative Library Services Division, Joint Committee on Institutional Libraries. College Park, Md.: American Correc-tional Association, 1975. pp. 3–4.

Covers the role of the library, materials collection, services, and fa-cilities in correctional institutions.

Type of literature:	Standards
Subject heading(s):	Libraries, Children's—
	Institutional—Standards

167 "Library Usage by Students and Young Adults" by Philip S. Wilder, Jr. Indiana Library Studies Report 4. Bloomington, Ind.: Graduate Library School, 1970. 34p. ED 046 472.

Examines the uses of and attitudes toward public, school, and aca-demic libraries by children and young adults using those facilities. Reports that (1) children younger than age thirteen accounted for 10 percent of the youth users of all libraries, 2 percent for the cen-tral libraries in large systems, 7 percent for medium-sized libraries, and 20 percent for small libraries, (2) 33 percent of the grade school students used the library several times a week, 28 percent weekly, 30 percent several times a month, and 8 percent once a month or less, and (3) public libraries were viewed by elementary students as more satisfactory for school-related use than their school libraries.

Type of literature:	Report—Research
Funding source(s):	Indiana State Library
Research method(s):	Questionnaire

Subject heading(s):   Libraries, Children's—User
                        Studies—Indiana

168   *Library Work with Children: Reprints of Papers and Addresses*, se-
          lected and annotated by Alice I. Hazeltine. Classics of Ameri-
          can Librarianship series, ed. by Arthur E. Bostwick. New York:
          H. W. Wilson, 1917. 396p. Illus. LCCN 17-26973.
Brings together papers representing the growth and trends of library
work with children from 1876 to 1911, including papers by the following writers: William Isaac Fletcher, Caroline Maria Hewins, Alice M. Jordon, Emily S. Hanaway, Mary Wright Plummer, Caroline
Mathews, and Henry Eduard Legler. Provides glimpses of children's
librarians' roots and the realization that librarians' professional concerns, such as developing children's interest in reading, and librarians' relationships with other community agencies, are not new ones.
          Type of literature: Essays
          Subject heading(s):   Libraries, Children's—History

169   *The Library's Public* by Bernard Berelson. A Report of the Pub-
          lic Library Inquiry. New York: Columbia University Press,
          1949. Repr.: Westport, Conn.: Greenwood Press, 1949. 174p.
          LCCN 49-10661.
Reports that children use the library more than adults and that children younger than age fifteen account for approximately 43 percent
of the circulation. However, libraries retain "only a small part of its
younger users after they have entered adulthood" (p. 22).
          Type of literature: Book—Research
          Funding source(s):   Carnegie Foundation
          Research method(s):   Survey
          Subject heading(s):   Libraries, Children's

170   "The Library's Responsibility to the Child" by Lillian H.
          Smith. In *The Library of Tomorrow: A Symposium*, pp. 124–
          32, ed. by Emily Miller Danton. Chicago: American Library
          Association, 1939.
Describes the changes children's librarians faced in the twenty years
preceding the essay's publication. Identifies the isolation children's
librarians feel, especially in small communities where the librarians
are removed from others holding similar positions. Observes that

"the important point to remember is that children's reading, unlike that of adults, is conditioned by what is at hand" (p. 125). Voices Smith's belief that the library's responsibility is to make books available.

Type of literature:	Essay—Opinion
Subject heading(s):	Librarians, Children's
	Libraries, Children's

171 "A Long-term Plan for Children's Services." Nebraska Library Commission, 1990. Unp.

Addresses the role parents and caregivers play in children's attitudes toward reading, and the role of children's librarians. Calls for programming throughout the year and discusses serving "children at risk." Outlines activities for each area to be completed between June 1990 and 1994.

Type of literature:	Report—Planning
Subject heading(s):	Librarians, Children's—Role
	Libraries, Children's—Planning—
	Nebraska

172 "LSCA Final Reports: Fourth Series," ed. by Collin Clark. Sacramento: California State Library, 1988. 203p. ED 304 155.

Includes summary reports on eight programs for children and youth funded by the Library Services and Construction Act and administered by the California State Library for the period of 1985–1987.

Type of literature:	Report
Funding source(s):	Library Services and Construction
	Act
Subject heading(s):	Libraries, Children's—Services—
	California

173 *Major Problems in the Education of Librarians*, ed. by Robert D. Leigh. New York: Columbia University Press, 1954. 116p. LCCN 54-6913.

Addresses the educational concerns for school and children's librarians, stating that "it is essential that the two systems of professional training bear some rational relationship to each other" (p. 68). Reports on a workshop at the University of Chicago in the summer of

1951 that recommends "that the basic formal training for children's and school librarians be the same, and that the undergraduate program in the teacher-training institutions include the professional education of both groups" (p. 75).

    Type of literature: Book—Opinion
    Subject heading(s):   Librarians, Children's—
                             Education

174   *Managers and Missionaries: Library Services to Children and Young Adults in the Information Age*, ed. by Leslie Edmonds. Papers presented at the Allerton Park Institute, sponsored by the University of Illinois Graduate School of Library and Information Science, co-sponsored by the youth divisions of the American Library Association (the American Association of School Librarians, the Association for Library Service to Children, and the Young Adult Services Division), held November 14–15, 1986, at the Chancellor Hotel and Conference Center, 15011 S. Neil, Champaign, Illinois. Allerton Park Institute series, no. 28. Champaign-Urbana: Graduate School of Library and Information Science, University of Illinois, 1989. 168p. ISBN 0-87845-075-0. ISSN 0536-4604.

Addresses the issues and challenges facing librarians serving youth and explores ways in which the sponsoring associations could help their members address those issues. Of particular relevance to this bibliography are the following chapters: "Changing Priorities for Service to Children and Adolescents in School and Public Libraries," by Marilyn Miller, pages 5–16; "The Right Stuff: Recruitment and Education for Children's and Young Adult Specialists," by Margaret Bush, pages 89–101; and "Evaluation and Measurement of Youth Services," by Gerald Hodges, pages 147–55.

    Type of literature: Conference Proceedings
    Subject heading(s):   Librarians, Children's—
                             Recruitment
                             Libraries, Children's—
                                  Conferences and Institutes—
                                  Proceedings
                             Libraries, Children's—Services

175 *Managing Children's Services in the Public Library* by Adele M. Fasick. Englewood, Colo.: Libraries Unlimited, 1991. 182p. ISBN 0-87287-643-8. LCCN 90-28689.
Describes the responsibilities of children's librarians for working within the department (planning, developing and using objectives, implementing policies, dealing with common problems, coping with censorship, organizing special events, creating a productive work environment), within the library system (communicating, preparing annual reports, preparing budgets, coordinating children's services, and planning facilities), and within the community (becoming visible, relating to school media centers, dealing with community agencies, working with other youth librarians). Describes real situations and offers practical advice and examples.

Type of literature:	Book—Opinion
Subject heading(s):	Libraries, Children's— Administration and Organization

176 "Marketing Children's Services at the Central Library of Sacramento Public Library" by Mary Frances Hicks. Master's Thesis, California State University, 1987. 159p. ED 283 532.
Assesses the need for children's services in downtown Sacramento. Profiles the community environment and general characteristics of the population and assesses family needs and desires for children's services. Determines that due to the small population of children in the downtown area, the central library staff must seek patrons outside that area.

Type of literature:	Master's Thesis
Research method(s):	Interviews
Subject heading(s):	Libraries, Children's—Central Library
	Sacramento Public Library

177 *Media Programs: District and School* by the American Association of School Librarians, ALA, and the Association for Educational Communications and Technology. Chicago: American Library Association; Washington, D.C.: Association for Educational Communications and Technology, 1975. 128p. ISBN 0-8389-3159-6.

Acknowledges that "it is unrealistic to claim that any school can provide within its own walls all of the materials and equipment that users need" (p. 62) and recommends that media staff obtain information and materials from other sources, such as the public library.

Type of literature:	Standards
Subject heading(s):	School and Public Libraries

178   *A Metropolitan Library in Action: A Survey of the Chicago Public Library* by Carleton Bruns Joeckel and Leon Carnovsky. Chicago: University of Chicago Press, 1940. 466p. LCCN 40-27038.

Describes the library in terms of organization, administration, and services in 1939. Traces the history of the library: (1) The children's department was established in 1907 in the central library, with a special reading room. (2) Between 1909 and 1920, story hours were introduced at the instigation of interested groups outside the library. (3) In 1909, a full-time children's librarian was appointed to one of the branches (Blackstone). (4) By 1928, children's work existed throughout the branch system. (5) In 1939, there was no general director for children's services (the central room staff had no administrative relationship to the Division of Work with Children in the Branch Department). Recommends a change in the organization of supervision.

Type of literature:	Book—Research
Research method(s):	Site Visits; Interviews
Subject heading(s):	Chicago Public Library—History
	Libraries, Children's—History

179   "Mildred L. Batchelder: A Study in Leadership" by Dorothy J. Anderson. Ph.D. Diss., Texas Woman's University, 1981. 383p. DAI 42/08A, p. 3332.

Covers Batchelder's national and international contributions to librarianship, her views about the profession (recruitment, library education, in-service needs), and how she confronted issues. Includes her service at ALA from 1936 to 1966 and the controversy when the American Association of School Librarians was founded. Includes comments from and correspondence with Association for Library Service to Children leaders during those years.

Type of literature:	Dissertation
Major professor:	Brooke Sheldon
Research method(s):	Interviews
Subject heading(s):	American Association of School Librarians—History
	Association for Library Service to Children—History
	Batchelder, Mildred L.— Biographies
	Librarians, Children's— Biographies
	Libraries, Children's—History

180 "The Mississippi Library Commission: A Force for Library Development" by Jeannine Lackey Loughlin. Ph.D. Diss., Indiana University, 1983. 221p. DAI 44/103A, p. 602.

Focuses on library development in the broad sense. Covers events relating to children's services, including the 1916 establishment of a combined school and public library in Natchez, the 1926 funding from the Carnegie Endowment for International Peace for the purchase and circulation of one hundred books about different countries for adults and children, the display of children's books by the Mississippi Library Commission at the 1929 State Fair, and the introduction of a statewide summer reading program in 1962.

Type of literature:	Dissertation
Research method(s):	Historical
Subject heading(s):	Libraries—History—Mississippi
	Mississippi Library Commission—History

181 "Multi-Purpose or Multi-Agency Libraries." Chicago: American Library Association, Library Administration Division, 1972. 18p.

Identifies forty-four school public libraries, listing their names, addresses, governing bodies, populations served, sponsoring agencies, funding, purposes, and square footages; and supplying comments about their hours and staff.

Type of literature:	Directory

Subject heading(s):   School and Public Libraries—
                             Directories

182   "National Survey of Support for Children's Services at the
          State Level" by Ethel Ambrose. *Public Libraries* 2:123–24
          (Winter 1981).
Reports that (1) fourteen state libraries called for a children's services specialist on their staff, but only five had full-time consultants;
(2) four states had standards for guidelines for children's services;
and (3) three others reported work on standards in progress. Notes
the lack of leadership for children's services in most state library
agencies.
          Type of literature: Article—Research
          Research method(s):   Questionnaire
          Subject heading(s):   Libraries, Children's—Standards
                                     Libraries, State
                                     Libraries, State—Consultants

183   "New Perspective on Cooperation in Library Services to Chil-
          dren" by Esther R. Dyer. *School Media Quarterly* 5:261–70
          (Summer 1977).
Discusses findings relating to the "survival of services to children,
the desirability of cooperation, the preferred means of coordination,
and the probable areas of successful cooperative programs" (p. 263).
Reports that 91 percent of the panelists questioned considered mul-
titype networking as the most desirable of cooperative programs and
58 percent considered it the most probable. Concludes that "panelists are apprehensive about the willingness of public schools and
public libraries to cooperate in the provision of services to children
as well as about these institutions' motives" (p. 269). Calls for active
planning and implementation of cooperation.
    Based on Dyer's dissertation "Cooperation in Library Services to
Children: A Fifteen-Year Forecast of Alternatives Using the Delphi
Technique."
          Type of literature: Article—Research
          Research method(s):   Delphi
          Subject heading(s):   School and Public Libraries

184 "Ohio Children's Services Surveyed by Task Force." *School Library Journal* 26:16–17 (Jan. 1980).

Announces the availability of *A Survey of Children's Services in Ohio Public Libraries 1979* (278). Highlights findings, including the facts that (1) children's librarians are involved in policy making for selection, programming, and promotion, but not for budget and personnel evaluation; (2) children's services receive a lower percentage of resources than the percentage of measurable results they provide to the library; and (3) most children's services are provided by bookmobiles. Concludes that conditions of understaffing and underfunding exist.

Type of literature:	Article—Research
Research method(s):	Questionnaire
Subject heading(s):	Libraries, Children's—Services—Ohio

185 "The Olney Experiment: A Venture in Coordination and Merger of School and Public Libraries" by James A. Kitchens. Denton: North Texas State University, 1981. 82p.

Assesses and evaluates the "coordinated library as it existed from its inception to the completion of the new building" (p. 1) in Olney, Texas, which has a population of 5,000. Concludes "we are dealing with an unusually successful approach to library services" (p. 2).

Type of literature:	Report—Research
Funding source(s):	United States Office of Education, Office of Libraries and Learning Resources
Research method(s):	Case Study; Interviews
Subject heading(s):	Olney Public Library
	School and Public Libraries

186 *The Organization and Administration of Library Service to Children* by Mary Rinehart Lucas. Master's Thesis, University of Chicago. Chicago: American Library Association, 1941. 108p.

Examines the place of library service to children in the organizational structure of the twelve public libraries serving populations of more than 200,000. Analyzes the organization patterns within the children's departments. Identifies the administrative relations between the staff responsible for service to children and other departments and agencies. Describes how the administrative functions required in service to children are performed, with particular reference to the groups of staff members concerned and to the tasks to which these functions apply. Covers four types of organization: advisory, cooperative, supervisory, and control.

Type of literature:	Master's Thesis
Research method(s):	Interviews
Subject heading(s):	Libraries, Children's— Administration and Organization

187   *Output Measures for Children's Services in Wisconsin Public Libraries* by Douglas L. Zweizig, Joan A. Braune, and Gloria A. Waity. Madison: School of Library and Information Studies, University of Wisconsin, 1989. 44p. ED 275 324.

Tests an adaptation of *Output Measures for Public Libraries* (189), which was used to measure children's services in Wisconsin's public libraries. Measures include juvenile circulation per juvenile capita, in-library use of juvenile materials per juvenile capita, juvenile library visits per juvenile capita, reference fill rates for juveniles, library registration of juveniles as a percentage of juvenile population, and turnover rate of juvenile materials.

Available for $5 from Publications Office, School of Library and Information Studies, University of Wisconsin-Madison, 600 N. Park St., Madison, WI 53706.

Type of literature:	Report—Research
Funding source(s):	Library Services and Construction Act
Research method(s):	Output Measures
Subject heading(s):	Libraries, Children's— Evaluation—Wisconsin Libraries, Children's—Services— Wisconsin

188   "Output Measures for Children's Services in Wisconsin Public Libraries" by Diana Young. *Public Libraries* 25:30–32 (Spring 1986).

Highlights the 1985 pilot study of the use of output measures for measuring children's services in Wisconsin. Describes the long-term effort in terms of meetings held to discuss the methodology, collection of data, data interpretation, sampling techniques, and positive reaction to the data collection experience.

Type of literature:	Article—Research
Research method(s):	Output Measures
Subject heading(s):	Libraries, Children's—Evaluation—Wisconsin
	Libraries, Children's—Services—Wisconsin

189 *Output Measures for Public Libraries: A Manual of Standardized Procedures*, prepared for the Public Library Development Project by Nancy A. Van House, Mary Jo Lynch, Charles R. McClure, Douglas L. Zweizig, and Eleanor Jo Rodger. 2nd ed. Chicago: American Library Association, 1987. 99p.

Defines output measures and the process of choosing them; describes managing the measurement effort; covers data collection, analysis, and reporting; presents ways to interpret and use the results; and describes measures relating to library use, materials use, materials access, reference services, and programming.

Type of literature:	Manual
Subject heading(s):	Libraries, Public—Evaluation

190 "Output Measures Identify Problems and Solutions for Middle Schoolers" by Cynthia M. Wilson. *Public Libraries* 29:19–22 (Jan.–Feb. 1990).

Adapts the fill rate survey format from *Output Measures for Public Libraries* (first edition) for use by middle-school children. Finds that (1) elementary school-age children made about seven annual visits per capita, while middle school-age children made fewer than three, (2) the subject/author fill rate for middle schoolers was 12 to 15 percent lower than for other library users, and (3) the turnover rate for fiction was lower for middle schoolers than for elementary-age children. Remedies the problems through a three-part program: (1) change the atmosphere and space resources, (2) weed and update the collection, and (3) use merchandising techniques, school visits, press releases, and other forms of promotion.

Type of literature:	Article—Research
Research method(s):	Output Measures; Questionnaire

Subject heading(s):   Children—Middle Schoolers
                        Libraries, Children's—Evaluation

191   "Parents and Teachers View Library Service to Children" by
          Adele Fasick. *Top of the News* 35:309–14 (Spring 1979).
Solicits librarians', parents', and teachers' rankings of types of services and materials that should be emphasized in planning for the
future by the South Central Regional Library System in Ontario. Reports the following to be considered more important by parents and
teachers than by librarians: (1) provision of nonbook materials, including magazines, cassettes, and filmstrips, (2) children's ability to
borrow from other libraries, and (3) provision of programs allowing
parents and children to participate together. Concludes that "many
parents and teachers agree with librarians that the traditional goals
of providing high-quality books for children, developing a love of
reading, holding storyhours, helping children to find information,
and guiding children in their book selection are still considered
among the library's most important tasks" (p. 313).
          Type of literature: Article—Research
          Research method(s):   Survey
          Subject heading(s):   Libraries, Children's—Services
                                  Libraries, Children's—User
                                      Studies
                                  South Central Regional Library
                                      System (Hamilton, Ontario,
                                      Canada)

192   "Persuasive Poster Power" by Jerry Watson, Marginell Powell
          Clayburn, and Bill Snider. *Catholic Library World* 56:423–26
          (May-June 1985).
Reports the results of a study to measure the effect of posters on children's selection of books from display tables, compared to books on
display without posters. Also included in the study was the display of
a collection of books by the poster illustrator to determine whether
children would seek out books illustrated by the poster artist. Reports that the quality of the graphic design of the posters and the
appeal to the intended age group influence selections. Recommends
the use of posters to motivate reluctant readers.
          Type of literature: Article—Research

Research method(s):   Experimental
Subject heading(s):   Libraries, Children's—Reading
                         Guidance
                         Posters

193   "The Philadelphia Project" by John Q. Benford. *Library Journal* 96:2041–7 (June 16, 1971).
Examines the "actual requirements for library resources by elementary and secondary grade students" (p.2041) and evaluates the resources in terms of these needs and national standards. Finds that resources and programs do not meet the expressed needs (about half of the students found what they needed). Identifies deterrents to using the library, such as too many rules and regulations, not getting help from libraries, fear of walking in the neighborhood, and crowded conditions.

Type of literature: Article—Research
Research method(s):   Survey; Interviews
Subject heading(s):   Libraries, Children's—
                         Collections—Evaluation
                         Libraries, Children's—Services—
                         Evaluation
                         Libraries, Children's—User
                         Studies
                         Philadelphia, Free Library of
                         User Studies

194   "Philosophy of Public Library Children's Services" by Faith H. Hektoen. Hartford: Connecticut State Library, 1981. 30p. ED 203 886.
Discusses Connecticut's need for a philosophy of public library services to children. Identifies needs of children and problems in library services and reviews literature on the philosophy of library services to children.

Type of literature: Position Paper
Subject heading(s):   Libraries, Children's—
                         Philosophy—Connecticut

195   "Philosophy of Public Library Children's Services: Part I" and
          "Part II" by Faith Hektoen. *Public Libraries* 21:22–26 (Spring
          1982) and 21:62–65 (Summer 1982), respectively.
Discusses Connecticut's need for a philosophy of public library services to children. Identifies improvements needed in Connecticut's
library services in the areas of collections, cooperative efforts among
agencies and institutions, reference and advisory services, programming, and continuing education for librarians. Part II includes a
bibliographic essay.

Type of literature:	Article—Opinion
Subject heading(s):	Librarians, Children's—
	Education
	Libraries, Children's—
	Philosophy—Connecticut

196   "Philosophy Statement: Library Services for the Gifted and
          Talented" by the Library Service to Children with Special
          Needs Committee, Association for Library Service to Chil-
          dren. *Top of the News* 38:301–2 (Summer 1982).
Notes that the major objective of library service to the gifted and
talented is to meet the individual needs of each child in the manner
and to the degree that is in harmony with his or her capabilities.
Identifies the environmental opportunities provided by a library to
gifted and talented children.

Type of literature:	Position Paper
Subject heading(s):	Children—Gifted
	Libraries, Children's—Philosophy

197   "Picture Books: What Do Reviews Really Review?" by John
          Warren Stewig. *Top of the News* 37:83–84 (Fall 1980).
Compares reviews in *Horn Book, Booklist, School Library Journal,* and
Bulletin of the Center for Children's Books in terms of attention given
to the visual qualities of the books. Calls for reviewers to review the
artwork in picture books.

Type of literature:	Article—Research
Research method(s):	Content Analysis
Subject heading(s):	Reviews and Reviewing

198　　"Pittsburgh's Beginning with Books Project" by Jill L. Locke. *Library Journal* 34:22–24 (Feb. 1988).

Describes the favorable effects on literacy activities and family reading patterns when 1,000 free packets of children's books were distributed to disadvantaged families. Notes that initially the well baby clinics of the Allegheny County Health Department were used as the distribution points until the Carnegie Library of Pittsburgh became officially affiliated with the project.

　　　　Type of literature:　　Article—Research
　　　　Research method(s):　　Questionnaire
　　　　Subject heading(s):　　Children—Disadvantaged
　　　　　　　　　　　　　　Libraries, Children's—Services—
　　　　　　　　　　　　　　　Pittsburgh
　　　　　　　　　　　　　　Pittsburgh, Carnegie Library of

199　　*Planning and Role Setting for Public Libraries: A Manual of Options and Procedures*, prepared for the Public Library Development Project by Charles R. McClure, Amy Owen, Douglas L. Zweizig, Mary Jo Lynch, and Nancy A. Van House. Chicago: American Library Association, 1987. 117p. ISBN 0-8389-3341-6. LCCN 87-11445.

Provides guidelines for the planning process, including gathering information, developing roles and missions, writing goals and objectives, managing and monitoring implementation, writing the planning document, and reviewing the results. Uses a program for preschoolers as an example for developing roles and missions, denoting the description, benefits, critical resources, and output measures to explore.

　　　　Type of literature:　　Manual
　　　　Subject heading(s):　　Libraries, Public—Goals and
　　　　　　　　　　　　　　　Objectives
　　　　　　　　　　　　　　Libraries, Public—Planning

200　　"Planning for Children's Services in Public Libraries" by Robin R. Gault and the Public Library Association Committee on Service to Children. *Public Libraries* 25:60–62 (Summer 1988).

Identifies ways children's services can be taken into account when using PLA's *Planning Process*. Suggests a community profile, surveys,

library statistics, and performance measures. Offers questions to use
to analyze the data.

        Type of literature: Article—Opinion
        Subject heading(s):   Libraries, Children's—
                                      Administration and
                                      Organization

201   *Planning for Excellence: A Checklist for Connecticut Public Libraries* by the Connecticut Service Measures Task Force. Hartford: Connecticut State Library, 1986. 91p.

Covers planning goals, objectives, and evaluation; budgets; personnel; services; programs; materials and equipment; and facilities for children's services. Appendixes include a reprint of "Philosophy of Public Library Children's Services: Part I" (195), by Faith Hektoen.

        Type of literature: Report—Planning
        Funding source(s):   Library Services and Construction
                                        Act
        Subject heading(s):   Libraries, Children's—Planning—
                                      Connecticut
                                      Libraries, Children's—Services

202   "Policies and Practices Affecting Juvenile Collections in County and Regional Libraries in Washington State" by Mae Benne. Seattle: School of Librarianship, University of Washington [1969]. 100p. Mimeographed.

Describes thirteen county and regional library districts, their development since 1934, and their policies dealing with selection, budgets for multiple copies, replacements, maintenance, rotation of collections, and limiting access. Recommends written selection policies and identifies the children's coordinator as having the responsibility for selecting materials, budgeting for new and replacement titles, purchasing paperback editions, adding nonprint materials, reevaluating and weeding the collections, rotating the collections, and offering in-service education.

        Type of literature: Report—Research
        Research method(s):   Interviews; Questionnaire
        Subject heading(s):   Libraries, Children's—Collec-
                                        tions—Washington (State)
                                      Libraries, Children's—Policies

203   *Practical Administration of Public Libraries* by Joseph L. Wheeler and Herbert Goldhor. New York: Harper & Row, 1962. 371p. LCCN 62-13767/L.
Devotes chapter 21 to the "Administration of Children's Services," covering history, organization, staffing, selection, programs, individual guidance, reference service, and story hours. Describes current problems and trends, including the development of school libraries, the use of mass media in libraries, and trends in education.

Type of literature:	Book—Opinion
Subject heading(s):	Libraries, Children's— Administration and Organization
	Libraries, Children's—History

204   "Preferences of Elementary-School Children for Subject-Heading Form" by Eloise Rue. Master's Thesis, Graduate Library School, University of Chicago, 1946. 190p.
Examines the preferences of 2,000 children (grades four through eight) for subject-heading form (compound heading, phrase, inverted heading, subheading, subdivision of a place, and national adjectival form). Identifies the factors influencing preference: age, IQ level, practice in the use of the catalog, terms used in the course of study, race, economic and social class, and the use of punctuation in heading form. Reports that children prefer phrases, simple headings, or known scientific terms.

Type of literature:	Master's Thesis
Research method(s):	Questionnaire; Observation
Subject heading(s):	Libraries, Children's—Cataloging
	Libraries, Children's—User Studies

205   *Principles for Planning Children's Services in Public Libraries in Michigan.* Lansing: Michigan Library Association, Children's Services Division, 1988. 29p. Three-hole punched.
Identifies principles of services to children in terms of their relation to library administration. Identifies competencies for entry-level librarians, experienced librarians, and librarians who coordinate or supervise the work of children's library services. Appendixes include recommended facilities.

Type of literature:　　　Guidelines
Subject heading(s):　　　Librarians, Children's—
　　　　　　　　　　　Competencies
　　　　　　　　　　　Libraries, Children's—Facilities
　　　　　　　　　　　Libraries, Children's—
　　　　　　　　　　　Guidelines—Michigan

206　*Principles of Children's Services in Public Libraries* by Mae
　　　Benne. Chicago: American Library Association, 1991. 332p.
　　　ISBN 0-8359-0555-2. LCCN 90-47427.
Uses illustrative goals and objectives statements to address the role
of children's librarians as managers and planners. Offers theory and
practical suggestions relating to services, collections, facilities, and
staffing. Devotes one chapter to children's services in rural systems.
Provides sample budget and programming forms.
　　　　Type of literature:　　　Book—Opinion
　　　　Subject heading(s):　　　Librarians, Children's
　　　　　　　　　　　　　Libraries, Children's—
　　　　　　　　　　　　　Administration and
　　　　　　　　　　　　　Organization
　　　　　　　　　　　　　Libraries, Children's—Goals and
　　　　　　　　　　　　　Objectives
　　　　　　　　　　　　　Libraries, Children's—Rural

207　"Print Dominates Library Service to Children" by Robert
　　　Grover and Mary Kevin Moore. *American Libraries* 13:268–
　　　69 (April 1982).
Reports the findings of a survey in which phonodiscs and audio
cassettes were the most frequently found form of nonprint media
included in children's collections in California. Notes that the study
results suggest that libraries in larger communities tend to offer
varied multimedia programs, such as story hours and films, more
frequently than libraries in smaller communities. Recommends in-
service education programs on nonprint media and services, as well
as courses in library schools dealing with the selection and use of
multimedia materials and technology.
　　　　Type of literature:　　　Article—Research
　　　　Research method(s):　　　Questionnaire

Subject heading(s): Librarians, Children's—
Education
Libraries, Children's—
Collections—California
Libraries, Children's—Programs
and Activities—California

208 "Professional Striving and the Orientation of Public Librarians toward Lower Class Clients" by Margaret Mary Kimmel. Ph.D. Diss., University of Pittsburgh, 1989. 166p. DAI 41/12A, p. 4873.

Tests whether librarians' search for a better image—for more status and prestige—was related to a regard for lower class clients. Recommends that younger and newer staff members receive encouragement when working with lower class patrons. Concludes that the high rate of loss of staff after ten years of service calls for library directors to make efforts to retain experienced staff and to redirect service priorities.

Type of literature: Dissertation
Research method(s): Questionnaire
Subject heading(s): Attitude Studies
Librarians, Children's

209 *Programming for Children with Special Needs* by the Association for Library Service to Children. ALSC Program Support Publications, no. 2. Chicago: American Library Association, 1981. 6p. ISBN 0-8389-5588-6.

Offers guidelines for philosophy, criteria, procedures, personnel, facilities, programming, and suggested resources for working with children with special needs.

Type of literature: Guidelines
Subject heading(s): Children—Disabled
Libraries, Children's—Guidelines

210 "Proposition 13: Effects on Library Services to Youth" by Carol Starr and Elizabeth Talbot. *Top of the News* 36:152–56 (Winter 1980).

Provides statistics on cutbacks in operating hours, staff, budgets, services, and collections of libraries resulting from the Proposition 13 tax reform initiative in California. Describes the impact on librarians, collections, and services. Reports that librarians' attitudes did not change toward their clientele.

Type of literature:	Article—Research
Research method(s):	Questionnaire
Subject heading(s):	Librarians, Children's
	Libraries, Children's—Services—
	California

211   *Public Libraries in the United States of America, Part I, 1876 Report.* Champaign-Urbana: Graduate School of Library Science, University of Illinois, 1965. 1,187p. Reprint of *Public Libraries in the United States of America: Their History, Condition, and Management: Special Report, Part I* by the Department of the Interior, Bureau of Education. Washington, D.C.: Government Printing Office, 1876. LCCN 71-25544.

Discusses issues faced in 1876, including the use of libraries by the young (chapter 18), noting that some libraries required a young person to be twelve or fourteen years old to use the materials. The report recommends no age restrictions. Describes the public library's relationship to the schools, and the types of materials that should be available in public libraries.

Type of literature:	Report
Subject heading(s):	Libraries, Children's

212   *Public Library and School Library Organizational Relationships and Interlibrary Cooperation: A Policy Statement* by the Wisconsin Department of Public Instruction. Madison, Wis.: Department of Public Instruction, 1976. 5p.

Describes school and public libraries in terms of authority for establishment, purpose of the programs, services offered, and provision of materials. Identifies specific areas for cooperative efforts.

Type of literature:	Policy
Subject heading(s):	Libraries—Cooperation
	School and Public Libraries—
	Policies

213 "The Public Library and the Latchkey Problem: A Survey" by Frances Smardo Dowd. *School Library Journal* 35:19–24 (July 1989).

Relates the results of research dealing with the role of public libraries in serving latchkey children. Reports the estimated number of latchkey children present in public libraries, a description of public library situations due to the presence of latchkey children, why the public library is used for latchkey children in lieu of child care, the status of policies and procedures relating to latchkey children, and the content and inclusions of library policies and procedures for latchkey children. Recommends education for librarians about the appropriate services for latchkey children, distribution of policies to the public, and involvement in community-sponsored committees addressing latchkey children.

Type of literature:	Article—Research
Funding source(s):	Texas Woman's University, New Faculty Research Grant
Research method(s):	Questionnaire
Subject heading(s):	Children—Latchkey
	Librarians, Children's—Education
	Libraries, Children's—Policies
	Libraries, Children's—Services

214 "Public Library Children's Services: Two Studies" by Maxine La Bounty. *Library Trends* 12:29–37 (July 1963).

Compares *Children's Services in Public Libraries: Organization and Administration* by Elizabeth Henry Gross with the collaboration of Gener I. Namovicz, 1963 (049) and *The Organization and Administration of Library Service to Children* by Mary R. Lucas, 1941 (186) in terms of the background of the studies and their reports on the organization, administration, personnel, and services of children's libraries.

Type of literature:	Article—Opinion
Subject heading(s):	Libraries, Children's—Research
	Libraries, Children's—Services

215 *The Public Library in the United States* by Robert D. Leigh. General Report of the Public Library Inquiry. New York: Columbia University Press, 1950. 272p.

Reports that juveniles borrow more than half the books that public libraries circulate each year and that more of them hold library registration cards than do adults. Views children's services as an impressive achievement.

Type of literature:	Book—Research
Funding source(s):	Carnegie Foundation
Research method(s):	Survey
Subject heading(s):	Libraries, Children's

216 *Public Library Service to Children* by Elizabeth H. Gross. Dobbs Ferry, N.Y.: Oceana Publications, 1967. 152p. LCCN 67-24347.

Traces the history of children's services and children's literature. Calls for public librarians to take courses in child psychology, reading instruction, and school curriculum, and to obtain knowledge of civic, political, economic, and social matters as they relate to library service and the administration of a children's room. Addresses recruitment.

Type of literature:	Book—Opinion
Subject heading(s):	Librarians, Children's— Education
	Libraries, Children's

217 *Public Library Service to Children: Foundation and Development* by Harriet G. Long. Metuchen, N.J.: Scarecrow Press, 1969. 162p. ISBN 8108-0291-0.

Traces the development of public library service to children in the context of the political, social, and economic environment from Colonial America through 1914. The final two chapters trace the development of the Cleveland Public Library and its services to children through 1914. Includes the early training programs for children's librarians and quotes from leading advocates of children's services.

Type of literature:	Book—Opinion
Subject heading(s):	Cleveland Public Library— History
	Librarians, Children's— Education
	Libraries, Children's

218 "Public Library Service to Children in Oklahoma" by Mary
Ann Wentroth. Paper presented at the general council meeting of the International Federation of Library Associations.
Washington, D.C., November 1974. Oklahoma City: Oklahoma State Department of Libraries, 1974. 14p. ED 105 833.
Highlights the use of federal funds for the multicounty library
operations in Oklahoma, including services to children. Identifies
activities of the Oklahoma Department of Libraries in terms of workshops, establishing standards for juvenile collections, and interlibrary loans.

Type of literature:	Article—Opinion
Subject heading(s):	Libraries, Children's—Services—
	Oklahoma
	Oklahoma Department of
	Libraries

219 *Public Library Services for Children* by Barbara T. Rollock. Hamden, Conn.: Shoe String Press, 1988. 228p. ISBN 0-208-02-
16-0. LCCN 88-12863.
Includes a historical overview of library services for children; reviews
four major studies about public library services; examines the exter-
nal and internal environments; and reports on library activities and
programs.

Type of literature:	Book—Opinion
Subject heading(s):	Libraries, Children's—
	Administration and
	Organization

220 "Public Library Services for Young Children: What Early
Childhood Educators Recommend" by Frances A. Smardo.
Children Today 9:24–27 (May-June 1980).
Presents the results of a study in which recommendations from early
childhood educators regarding library work with young children
were obtained. The data were used to develop guidelines for public
libraries, including services, programs, materials, physical facilities,
and the training and use of personnel.

Type of literature:	Article—Research
Research method(s):	Questionnaire; Interview

Subject heading(s):   Librarians, Children's—
                                    Education
                       Libraries, Children's—Guidelines
                       Libraries, Children's—Services

221 "Public Library Services to Preschool Children" by Joyce
         Williams Bergin. Master's Thesis, Texas Woman's University,
         1984. 45p. ED 275 345.
Reports that those providing library services to preschoolers lack
preparation in early childhood services and that such services hold
a low priority for Texas libraries.
         Type of literature: Master's Thesis
         Research method(s):   Questionnaire
         Subject heading(s):   Children—Preschoolers
                                Librarians, Children's—
                                    Education
                                Libraries, Children's—Services—
                                    Texas

222 "Public Library Services to Visually Disabled Children in the
         United States" by Santi Gopal Basu. Ph.D. Diss., Florida State
         University, 1987. 189p. DAI 48/12A, p. 3001.
Finds that (1) special services and equipment are offered in subre-
gional libraries of the National Library Service for the Blind and
Physically Handicapped more than in public libraries and (2) there
is no relationship between the size of a library and its offering of
general and special library services to visually disabled children.
         Type of literature: Dissertation
         Research method(s):   Questionnaire
         Subject heading(s):   Children—Handicapped
                                Libraries, Children's—
                                    Services

223 "Putting Theory into Practice: MBO and PM Have Their Day"
         by Carol Batty. *Illinois Libraries* 64:1171–75 (Dec. 1982).
Reports the successful application of Management by Objectives
(MBO) and Participatory Management (PM) techniques by the children's department at the Champaign (Illinois) Public Library. Includes goals, objectives, and evaluation statements.

Type of literature: Policy
Subject heading(s):   Libraries, Children's—
                                 Administration and
                                 Organization
                             Libraries, Children's—Goals and
                                 Objectives

224   "Reaching All Children: A Public Library Dilemma" by Alice
          Phoebe Naylor. *Library Trends* 35:369–92 (Winter 1987).
Describes populations of concern to children's services over the past
twenty-five years. Analyzes entries used in *Library Literature* between
1960 and 1985. Compares the coverage of minority groups in articles
in *School Library Journal, Top of the News, Wilson Library Bulletin*, and
Public Libraries.
          Type of literature: Article—Research
          Research method(s):   Content Analysis; Interviews
          Subject heading(s):   Children—Minority
                                       Libraries, Children's—Services

225   "Reaching for Tomorrow Today" by Diana Young. *Public Li-
          braries* 19:119–21 (Winter 1980).
Announces the availability of the Ohio Library Association's *A Survey
of Children's Services in Ohio Public Libraries 1979* (278). Provides the
executive summary and conclusions covering services, administration, staff, materials, programs, and procedures.
          Type of literature: Article—Research
          Research method(s):   Questionnaire
          Subject heading(s):   Libraries, Children's—Services—
                                       Ohio

226   *Reader in Children's Librarianship*, ed. by Joan Foster. Read-
          ers in Librarianship and Information Science, no. 27. Engle-
          wood, Colo.: Information Handling Services, 1978. 450p.
          Illus. ISBN 0-910972-89-3.
Presents a diversity of viewpoints and addresses the paradox of how
some people value children's librarians and others consider them
to hold low positions. Includes both research and opinion pieces.
Recommends additional readings for many of the sections.
          Type of literature: Essays

Subject heading(s):   Librarians, Children's
                        Libraries, Children's

227   "Realistic Guidelines?" by Diana Young. *Public Libraries*
          19:31–32 (Spring 1980).
Highlights guidelines for two rural states, Vermont and Virginia,
covering philosophy, staff, budget, materials, physical facilities, programming, and the role of trustees.
          Type of literature: Standards
          Subject heading(s):   Libraries, Children's—
                                      Standards—Vermont
                                  Libraries, Children's—
                                      Standards—Virginia

228   *Realities: Educational Reform in a Learning Society.* Chicago:
          American Library Association, 1984. 13p.
Responding to *A Nation at Risk: The Imperative for Educational Reform*,
the American Library Association Task Force recommends: (1) state
aid for public libraries should be increased, (2) library statistical data
and planning information must be assumed by the National Center
for Education Statistics, (3) librarians should be included in planning and program development by local, state, and federal agencies
developing human services and education programs, and (4) "librarians, library boards, friends of libraries, parents, and educators
should consider the recommendations which resulted from the *Libraries and the Learning Society* seminars sponsored by the U.S. Department of Education, and they should implement those which are
needed to reshape and improve library services" (p. 12).
          Type of literature: Report—Opinion
          Subject heading(s):   Libraries, Children's

229   "Reference Service in the Children's Department: A Case
          Study" by Janice N. Harrington. *Public Library Quarterly* 6:65–
          75 (Fall 1985).
Analyzes reference and information requests according to types of
questions and patrons (adult, child, young adult) making the requests. Reports that adults ask directional and advisory questions;
children and young adults ask for materials and ask locational and

library instruction questions. Finds that 20 percent of the queries at the children's services department were from adults.

> Type of literature: Article—Research
> Research method(s): Reference Queries—Analysis
> Subject heading(s): Libraries, Children's—Reference Services

230 "Reference Work with Children" by Harriet H. Stanley. *Library Journal* 26:74–78 (Aug. 1901).

Reports that children usually asked questions related to their school work, although some personal inquiries were related to sports, mechanical occupations, and pets. Offers suggestions for teachers in assigning reference work, and describes how public librarians are working with schoolchildren.

> Type of literature: Article—Research
> Research method(s): Survey
> Subject heading(s): Libraries, Children's—Reference Services

231 "Remembering *Top of the News*" by Holly Willett. *Journal of Youth Services in Libraries* 2:127–35 (Winter 1989).

Highlights the experiences, perceptions, and backgrounds of seven of the editors who served during the period of 1942 to 1966 and who worked with Mildred Batchelder, the association's executive director.

> Type of literature: Article—Research
> Subject heading(s): Association for Library Service to Children—Periodicals
> *Top of the News*

232 *Report of Contemplation of Children's Services in Public Libraries of Wisconsin* by the Wisconsin State Department of Public Instruction. Madison: Wisconsin State Department of Public Instruction, Division of Library Services, 1979. 137p. ED 196 445.

Reports the activities of a two-day workshop designed to plan for the assessment, examination, and evaluation of public library services to children in the state. States that groups addressed guidelines, data collection, annual allocations of Library Services and Construction

Act funds, methods of exchange of information, and the implications of computerization and technology.

  Type of literature: Report—Planning
  Subject heading(s): Libraries, Children's—Planning—
           Wisconsin
           Libraries, Children's—Services—
           Wisconsin

233 *A Report of the First Statewide Survey of Children's Services in Public Libraries of Wisconsin.* Madison: Wisconsin Department of Public Instruction, 1981. 53p. ED 212 259.

Finds that children's library services were strong in the areas of informational requests, materials access, summer library programming, and continuing education for staff and weak in the areas of management, administration, and collection development. Identifies the lack of proportional relationship between the percentage of children's materials circulated and the budget, staff, and space allotted to them in Wisconsin's public libraries. Reports that about one-third of the libraries limited the number of items a child may borrow at one time and that only 47 percent of the children's areas were accessible to the handicapped.

  Type of literature: Report—Research
  Research method(s): Survey
  Subject heading(s): Libraries, Children's—Services—
           Wisconsin

234 "Research in Children's Services in Public Libraries: A Group Project in North Carolina" by Karen Perry. *Public Libraries* 19:58–60 (Summer 1980).

Describes the reasons a child or parent was attracted to a library activity for the first time and whether the child continues to use the library. Notes children's dependency on adults for transportation.

  Type of literature: Article—Research
  Research method(s): Interviews
  Subject heading(s): Libraries, Children's—Services—
           North Carolina

235 "Research on Children's Services in Libraries: An Annotated Bibliography" by Marion F. Gallivan. *Top of the News* 30:275–93 (April 1974).

Covers publications from 1960 through the fall of 1972, describing their methodologies, subjects, and findings. Identifies sources of information about research projects.

Type of literature: Article—Bibliography
Subject heading(s): Libraries, Children's—Research—
Bibliographies

236 "Research on Library Services for Children and Young Adults: Implications for Practice" by Shirley Fitzgibbons. *Emergency Librarian* 9:6–17 (May-June 1982).

Describes the conclusions of approximately fifty-eight research studies from the period of 1970 to 1981. Recommends areas for further research.

Type of literature: Article—Bibliography
Subject heading(s): Libraries, Children's—Research—
Bibliographies

237 "Research: The How and Why of It," ed. by Adele Fasick and Shirley Fitzgibbons. Theme Issue. *Top of the News* 37:127–56 (Winter 1981).

Includes papers presented at the preconference in 1980 sponsored by the Association for Library Service to Children, the Young Adult Services Division, and the Public Library Association. Presenters were Jane Robbins Carter on "Practical Research for Practicing Librarians," Mary Jo Lynch on "Costing Small-Scale Research," and W. Boyd Rayward on "Reporting the Results of Library Research: To Inform Others, to Improve Practice, and to Add to Knowledge in the Field."

Type of literature: Article—Opinion
Subject heading(s): Libraries, Children's—Research

238 "Researching Children's Services in Public Libraries," ed. by Faith H. Hektoen. *School Library Journal* 26:21–27 (April 1980).

Highlights investigations by Faith Hektoen on "The Connecticut Research Documentation Project," Janet Gourley and Nancy DeSalvo on "Parent Support Services in Glastonbury and Farmington" (Connecticut), Diana Norton and Laurel Goodgion on "Documenting Information Requests," and Mae Benne on "Information Services in Central Children's Libraries."

    Type of literature: Article—Research
    Subject heading(s):   Libraries, Children's—Research

239   *Rich the Treasure: Public Library Service to Children* by Harriet
        G. Long. Chicago: American Library Association, 1953. 78p.
        LCCN 53-9660.

Identifies the goals of library service to children: "1. To make a wide and varied collection of books easily and temptingly available. 2. To give guidance to children in their choice of books and materials. 3. To share, extend and cultivate the enjoyment of reading as a voluntary, individual pursuit. 4. To encourage lifelong education through the use of public library resources. 5. To help the child develop to the full his personal ability and his social understanding. 6. To serve as a social force in the community together with other agencies concerned with the child's welfare" (p. 15). Addresses the educational needs of children's librarians. The book is cited frequently in the literature for the statement of goals.

    Type of literature: Book—Opinion
    Subject heading(s):   Librarians, Children's—
                        Education
                      Libraries, Children's—Goals and
                        Objectives
                      Libraries, Children's—Services

240   "The Role of the Children's Librarian as a Professional Librarian: A Position Paper" by Bessie Egan. *Emergency Librarian*
        7–8:13–16 (May-June 1981).

Describes the historical development of education for children's librarians, the current conditions, and the competencies needed. Includes a job description.

    Type of literature: Position Paper
    Subject heading(s):   Librarians, Children's—
                        Competencies
                      Librarians, Children's—
                        Education

Librarians, Children's—Job
Descriptions

241 "School and Public Library Collection Overlap and the Implications for Networking" by Carol A. Doll. *School Library Media Quarterly* 11:193–99 (Spring 1983).
Highlights the findings from Doll's dissertation "A Study of Overlap and Duplication among Children's Collections in Public and Elementary School Libraries" and reports on related studies.

Type of literature:	Article—Research
Research method(s):	Collection Analysis
Subject heading(s):	Libraries, Children's—Collections
	Networking
	School and Public Libraries

242 *Selected Proceedings of a Special Study Institute on Improving Library Services for Handicapped Children (Buffalo, New York, February 1–4, 1971)* by the New York State Education Department, Albany, Division for Handicapped Children. Buffalo: School of Information and Library Studies, State University of New York, 1971. 83p. ED 054 779.
Covers improving library services to handicapped children in terms of media, the use of libraries by exceptional children, library materials, school library programs, cooperation, programmed reading materials, audiovisual aids, and Braille.

Type of literature:	Report—Institute
Subject heading(s):	Children—Handicapped
	Libraries, Children's—
	Conferences and Institutes—
	Proceedings
	Libraries, Children's—Services

243 "Selected Research Related to Children's and Young Adult Services in Public Libraries" by Marilyn Louise Shontz. *Top of the News* 38:125–42 (Winter 1982).
Summarizes sixty research studies that addressed public library services and use. Compares topics before 1970 with those addressed later. Identifies research needs.

Type of literature:	Bibliography

Subject heading(s):   Libraries, Children's—Research—
                                          Bibliographies

244 *Self-Assessment Guide for Children's Services.* St. Paul, Minn.:
        Office of Library Development and Services, 1988. 87p.
Identifies roles and competencies needed as information provider,
programmer, collection developer, manager, networker, and advo-
cate, and in the areas of organizational and operational knowledge,
communication skills and attitudes, interpersonal skills and attitudes, professional attitudes, and personal traits. Annotated bibliography lists resources for continuing education.
        Type of literature: Guidelines
        Subject heading(s):   Librarians, Children's—
                                          Competencies
                                      Librarians, Children's—
                                          Continuing Education

245 "Service to Children in Groups" by Vicki Deljen and others.
        Public Libraries 25:100–4 (Fall 1986).
Presents the Hennepin County Library policy about the provision of
library services to children. Offers guidelines and identifies priorities
to carry out the policy.
        Type of literature: Policy
        Subject heading(s):   Hennepin County Library
                                      Libraries, Children's—Policies
                                      Libraries, Children's—Services

246 *Services and Resources for Children in Public Libraries, 1988–
        1989* by Laurie Lewis and Elizabeth Farris. Washington, D.C.:
        Government Printing Office, 1990. 42p. ED 320 610.
Reports on the first national survey of public library services to and
resources for children. Examines the (1) number of library users per
week, (2) type of library, (3) children's librarian, (4) hours open to
the public, (5) percentage of the book budget used for children's
books, and (6) percentage of the total circulation from children's
materials.
        Type of literature: Report—Research
        Research method(s):   Questionnaire

Subject heading(s):   Libraries, Children's—Collections
Libraries, Children's—Services

247   "Services and Resources in California Public Libraries in Fiscal Year 1977–1978 and Fiscal Year 1982–1983" by Holly Geneva Willett. Ph.D. Diss., University of North Carolina–Chapel Hill, 1986. 333p. DAI 48/01A, p. 241.
Examines the proportion of budget reduction for services to children and young adults in periods of budget retrenchment in terms of public service staffing, supervisors and coordinators, materials expenditures, volumes acquired, activity programs, outreach projects, and outreach project staff.

Type of literature: Dissertation
Major professor: Marilyn Miller
Research method(s):   Questionnaire; Case Studies
Subject heading(s):   Libraries, Children's—Budget
Libraries, Children's—California

248   "Serving Latchkey Children: Recommendations from Librarians" by Frances Smardo Dowd. *Public Libraries* 28:101–6 (March-April 1989).
Reports that ten-, eleven-, and twelve-year-olds most often used the library instead of child-care facilities. Describes programs and services being offered. Offers advice about services to latchkey children.

Type of literature: Article—Research
Research method(s):   Questionnaire; Interviews
Subject heading(s):   Children—Latchkey
Libraries, Children's—Services

249   *Sources of Library Statistics, 1972–1982* by Mary Jo Lynch. Chicago: American Library Association, 1983. 48p. ISBN 0-8389-3292-4.
Provides descriptive annotations for federal, public library, and commercial sources. The sources cover monies, materials, and personnel.

Type of literature: Bibliography
Subject heading(s):   Statistics, Library—Bibliographies

250 *South Carolina State Library Annual Report, 1988–1989.* Columbia: South Carolina State Library, 1989. 71p. ED 316 256.
Includes a report of children's consultants' activities and projects funded by the State Library (outreach programs to child-care centers and latchkey projects).

Type of literature:	Annual Report
Subject heading(s):	Libraries, Children's—Services— South Carolina
	Libraries, State—South Carolina

251 "Spanish-Language Books for Young Readers in Public Libraries: National Survey of Practices and Attitudes" by Isabel Schon, Kenneth D. Hopkins, and Marjorie Woodruff. *Journal of Youth Services in Libraries* 1:444–50 (Summer 1988).
Reports that (1) 89 percent of the libraries purchase books in Spanish, (2) personal examination is the highest influence on selection, and (3) librarians are strongly positive in their attitudes and practices regarding making books in Spanish available to children and young adults.

Type of literature:	Article—Research
Research method(s):	Questionnaire
Subject heading(s):	Attitude Studies
	Books—Spanish Language
	Libraries, Children's—Collections

252 *Special Collections in Children's Literature,* ed. by Carolyn W. Field. Chicago: American Library Association, 1982. 57p. Illus. ISBN 0-8389-0345-2.
Updates *Subject Collections in Children's Literature* (R. R. Bowker, 1969), which listed 133 institutions; the 1982 edition covers 267. Arranged by subject and including a directory of collections (United States listed by state; Canada, by province). Appendix I: "References to Collections" (articles, bibliographies, checklists, brochures, catalogs, etc.); Appendix II: "Authors and Illustrators in Major Collections Not Listed in Body of Work."

Type of literature:	Directory
Subject heading(s):	Libraries—Directories—Canada
	Libraries—Directories—United States

Literature, Children's—Special
Collections—Canada
Literature, Children's—Special
Collections—United States

253 *Standards and Guidelines for Florida Public Library Services*, ed.
by Alphonse F. Trezza. Winter Park: Florida Library Association, 1985. 38p.
Uses the Public Library Association's *Standards for Children's Services
in Public Libraries* (254), published in 1964, as a base for guidelines
covering personnel, materials, facilities, and services.

Type of literature: Standards
Subject heading(s):   Libraries, Children's—
            Standards—Florida

254 *Standards for Children's Services in Public Libraries* by the Subcommittee on Standards for Children's Service, Public Library Association, American Library Association. Chicago:
American Library Association, 1964. 24p. LCCN 64-24946.
Follows the pattern, philosophy, and definitions of the Public Library Association's *Public Library Service: A Guide to Evaluation, with
Minimum Standards* (1956) and refines those standards for library
systems. Identifies objectives, using those stated by Harriet G. Long
in *Rich the Treasure* (239). Addresses administration, personnel, services, materials, and physical facilities.

Type of literature: Standards
Subject heading(s):   Libraries, Children's—Standards

255 *Standards for Children's Services in Public Libraries of New York
State* by the Committee on Standards for Children's Services,
Children's and Young Adult Services Section, New York Library Association. Woodside: New York Library Association,
1967. 23p.
Covers the role of children's services, types of services, materials,
nonbook materials, physical facilities, and personnel. Combines
quantitative and qualitative standards. Reflects the diversity of the
size and structure of public libraries in New York State.

Type of literature: Standards

Subject heading(s):   Libraries, Children's—
                        Standards—New York State

256   *Standards for North Carolina Public Libraries,* a joint project
          of the Public Library Section of the North Carolina Library
          Association and the North Carolina Public Library Directors
          Association. N.p.: Ingram Library Services, Gaylord Brothers,
          Inc., and CLSI, Inc., 1988. 24p.
Combines input and output measures at three levels of standards (A,
B, and C) in the areas of administration, services, materials, public
relations, physical facilities, and personnel.

Type of literature: Standards
Funding source(s):   Ingram Library Services
                        Gaylord Brothers, Inc.
                        CLSI, Inc.
                        Library Services and Construction
                        Act
Subject heading(s):   Libraries, Children's—
                        Standards—North Carolina

257   *Standards for Public Library Services to Children in Massachu-
          setts.* Wakefield: Massachusetts Library Association, 1987.
          Unp.
Covers philosophy, services, staff, collections, programs, and facilities.

Type of literature: Standards
Subject heading(s):   Libraries, Children's—
                        Standards—Massachusetts

258   *Standards for Youth Services in Public Libraries of New York State*
          by the Task Force on Standards for Youth Services, Youth
          Services Section, New York Library Association. New York:
          New York Library Association, 1984. 28p.
Includes a philosophy of and an introduction to children's services.
Covers standards for children's services, including materials and
collections (print, nonprint, collection size, maintenance); services
(service to the community, reference services, programming, public relations); and facilities for children. Also includes standards for
young adult services. Separate sections deal with staffing, management, and the role of the youth specialist.

Available for $5 *plus* a mailing and handling fee (for one to five copies, the mailing and handling fee is $1; six to ten copies, $1.25; and bulk orders, $1.50) from the New York Library Association, 15 Park Row, Suite 434, New York, NY 10038.

> Type of literature: Standards
> Subject heading(s):   Libraries, Children's—
>   Standards—New York (State)

259   *State Education Documents: A State-by-State Directory for Their Acquisition and Use* by the Education-Related Government Publications Subcommittee, the Curriculum Materials Committee, and the Problems of Access and Control of Educational Materials Committee, Education and Behavioral Sciences Section, Association of College and Research Libraries, American Library Association. Chicago: American Library Association, 1989. 45p. ISBN 0-8389-7327-2.

Lists by state where to write for information (state agencies including the state library), types of materials published, their availability for purchase and to other states, depository programs, the availability of a checklist of publications, the use of commercial indexing or microfilming companies, microformat versions, municipal education documents, and sources of information.

> Type of literature: Bibliography
> Subject heading(s):   State Agencies—Bibliographies

260   "State Libraries Agencies—Are They Assuming a Leadership Role in Service to Children?" by Diana Young. *Public Libraries* 20:124–25 (Winter 1981).

Compares a 1956 survey by the Public Library Association's Service to Children Committee on state libraries with the Association of Specialized and Cooperative Library Agencies 1980 survey. Identifies trends in the decline in number of graduate librarians, the number of children's librarian positions being filled by professionals, the support of federal monies, travel budgets, materials budgets, and the purchasing power of the dollar. Finds that in 1980 44 percent of the state library agencies had a children's services consultant, with 22 percent of the consultants being full time and 37 percent of the consultants spending fewer than five days a week out in the state with their clientele.

Type of literature: Article—Research
Research method(s):   Questionnaire
Subject heading(s):   Libraries, State—Consultants

261   "The State Library Extension Agency and Services to Children" by Barbara Davis Widem. Master's Thesis, University of Chicago, 1957. 89p.

Surveys thirty-eight state library and agency programs designed to promote and develop services to children. Reports a lack of uniformity in the administration of these services and finds that twenty-five of the thirty-nine positions had responsibilities primarily for school libraries. Notes that services provided include materials lending (books, films, records), exhibits, collections weeding, and booklists.

Type of literature: Master's Thesis
Major professor: Margaret Hayes
Funding source(s):   E. P. Dutton—John Macrea Award
Research method(s):   Questionnaire
Subject heading(s):   Libraries, State—Services

262   "State Standards and Children's Services—One State's Efforts" by Jean B. Heath. *Public Libraries* 19:32–33 (Spring 1980).

Traces the development of Virginia's "Children's Services Guidelines," which covers staff, materials, access, planning and management, state consultants, and cooperation with other libraries and agencies.

Type of literature: Standards
Subject heading(s):   Libraries, Children's—
                         Standards—Virginia

263   *State Standards for Public Libraries* by Rose Vainstein and Marian Magg. U.S. Department of Health, Education and Welfare Bulletin, no. 22. Washington, D.C.: Government Printing Office, 1960. 85p.

Traces the development of state standards and describes the current ones.

Type of literature: Standards
Subject heading(s):   Libraries—Standards

264 "Statistics on Library Services to Youth" by Mary Jo Lynch. *Top of the News* 41:181–83 (Winter 1985).
Describes the National Center for Education Statistics project, the lack of statistics and possible sources, and actions that librarians and professional associations should take.

Type of literature:	Article—Opinion
Subject heading(s):	Libraries, Children's—Statistics

265 "Student's Attitudes toward Learning and Libraries" by George W. Huang. *California School Libraries* 47:34–40 (Fall 1975).
Reports the results of a study conducted with first through eighth grade students during the 1973–74 school year in five northern California counties. Finds that (1) the younger students liked reading and libraries more than the older children, (2) more of the girls than the boys liked reading and going to the library, and (3) more of the children preferred to go to their school libraries than to their public libraries.

Type of literature:	Article—Research
Research method(s):	Questionnaire
Subject heading(s):	Attitude Studies
	Libraries, Children's—User Studies

266 "A Study of Changes in Children's Library Services for Selected Pittsburgh Suburbs Related to Changes in Their Population for 1960 through 1970" by Jean D. Tower. Ph.D. Diss., University of Pittsburgh, 1972. 212p. DAI 33/08A, p. 4446.
Compares changes in both public and school library service for children in regard to resources, staffing, and financial allocation. Finds that services increased with increasing populations, but that staffing and financial allocations grew more rapidly for the school libraries than the public libraries.

Type of literature:	Dissertation
Research method(s):	Content Analysis
Subject heading(s):	Libraries, Children's—Services

267 *A Study of Combined School-Public Libraries* by Shirley L. Aaron. School Media Centers: Focus on Trends and Issues no. 6. Chicago: American Library Association, American Association of School Librarians, 1980. 107p. ISBN 0-8389-3249-9.

Reports on the three phases of the study. Phase 1: the development of an interview schedule and other evaluative instruments to gather relevant information about combination programs and visits to selected libraries in the United States and Canada. Phase 2: an analysis of past and current merger attempts in Florida. Phase 3: the development of a model procedure designed to help a community decide whether a combined library or another alternative would offer the best library services in its particular locality. Rates sites as successful or unsuccessful, recommending that libraries be developed within the context of total community services.

Highlights of phases 1 and 2 are described in "Combined School and Public Library Programs: An Abstract of a National Study" by Shirley L. Aaron. *School Media Quarterly* 7:31–32, 49–53 (Fall 1978). The full report is *A Study of the Combined School Public Library* by Shirley L. Aaron and Sue O. Smith. Tallahassee: School of Library Science, Florida State University, 1977–78.

Type of literature:	Report—Research
Research method(s):	Questionnaire; Interviews; Site Visits
Subject heading(s):	School and Public Libraries— Canada
	School and Public Libraries— Florida
	School and Public Libraries— United States

268   *A Study of Exemplary Public Library Reading and Reading-Related Programs for Children, Youth and Adults*, v. 1 and 2, by Barass, Reitzel, and Associates, Inc., Cambridge, Mass. Washington, D.C.: Department of Health, Education and Welfare, Office of Education, 1972. 612p. ED 066 197.

Presents case studies of thirty library reading and reading-related programs from 241 recommended programs. Of these, twenty were described as exemplary. Each of the thirty programs is described in terms of activities and procedures, materials, facilities, the role of volunteers, staff roles, and the relation to the community. Issues raised in the cases included the distance of outreach services from the regular library facility and how staff qualifications, acquisitions procedures, bookshelves, and distribution practices should be altered to encourage the participants in the reading program. Other issues included the library's responsibility to heed its advisory committee.

Type of literature:	Report—Research
Research method(s):	Case Studies
Subject heading(s):	Libraries, Children's—Services

269 "A Study of Overlap and Duplication among Children's Collections in Selected Public and Elementary School Libraries" by Carol A. Doll. Ph.D. Diss., University of Illinois, 1980. 196p. DAI 41/11A, p. 4528.

Finds (1) less overlap (two libraries owning the same title) between school libraries than between public libraries, (2) that as collection size increases, overlap increases, (3) that the greater the number of titles in a collection listed in selection aids, the greater the overlap, and (4) no apparent relationship between collection size and duplicate titles. This pattern was evident for books, magazines, science filmstrips, and fiction sound recordings.

Highlights reported in "A Study of Overlap and Duplication among Children's Collections in Selected Public and Elementary School Libraries." *Library Quarterly* 54:277–89 (July 1984).

Type of literature:	Dissertation
Major professor:	Selma K. Richardson
Research method(s):	Shelflist—Analysis; Questionnaire
Subject heading(s):	Libraries, Children's—Collections

270 *A Study of the Indianapolis-Marion County Public Library's Summer Reading Program for Children* by Edward L. Robbins and Linda W. Thompson. Final Report. Indianapolis: Measurement and Evaluation Center for Reading Education, Indiana University-Purdue University at Indianapolis, 1989. 18p. ED 316 845.

Reports that participants in the summer reading program maintained their reading achievement levels, read at least fifty books, read with others, and expressed positive attitudes about the program.

Type of literature: Report—Research
Research method(s):   Survey
Subject heading(s):   Libraries, Children's—Programs
                            and Activities
                         Summer Reading Programs

271   "A Study of the School/Public Library Concept: Summary,
          Conclusions, and Recommendations" by Wilma Lee Wool-
          ard. *Illinois Libraries* 60:281–89 (March 1978).
Reports that (1) libraries serving populations of fewer than 10,000
residents accounted for forty-two of the facilities in 1975, (2) the
lack of a school or public library was the greatest single factor for
the development of combined facilities, which often were located
in school attendance centers, and (3) twenty-three of the combined
libraries used two or more professional librarians. Identifies the benefits and advantages reported by the respondents.
          Type of literature: Article—Research
          Research method(s):   Survey; Questionnaire
          Subject heading(s):   School and Public Libraries

272   "A Study to Determine the Nature and Status of Children's
          Film Programs in Public Libraries of the Northeastern United
          States" by Daniel Lesser. Ed.D. Diss., Syracuse University,
          1963. 153p. DAI 24/12, p. 5422.
Reports that one out of six libraries offered film programs. The degree to which film programs were offered tended to be proportionate
to the size of the library system. Obstacles included inadequate finances and a shortage of equipment, space, and staff. Recommends
competencies needed by librarians, as few librarians had training
in film use. Reports that programs were striving to ally books and
children's films, rather than focusing on the entertainment value of
films. Finds that weaknesses in children's films were their overde-
scriptiveness and inadequate tempo.
          Type of literature: Dissertation
          Research method(s):   Questionnaire; Interviews
          Subject heading(s):   Films
                                   Libraries, Children's—Programs
                                      and Activities

273   *Summer Learning and the Effects of Schooling* by Barbara Heyns. New York: Academic Press, 1978. 326p. LCCN 76-3339.
Describes the impact of libraries in facilitating reading and, therefore, achievement. Assumes that libraries play a significant role in the achievement process because they shape children's use of the library in determinate ways, irrespective of the income or educational status of parents, and because they transmit parental status in different ways in the communities. Points out the difference of allocation of services to more advantaged children of white families and to disadvantaged black families.

Type of literature:	Book—Research
Research method(s):	Interviews
Subject heading(s):	Libraries, Children's—User Studies

274   "Support for Youth Services in a Period of Fiscal Retrenchment: California Public Libraries, 1977–78 and 1982–83" by Holly G. Willett. *Library and Information Science Research* 11:175–88 (April-June 1989).
Compares proportional relationships among services to children, young adults, and adults during these periods of retrenchment in California. Concludes that the findings both support and refute the belief that youth services received limited administrative support during budget crises.

Type of literature:	Article—Research
Funding source(s):	Bush Institute for Child and Family Policy
Research method(s):	Questionnaire; Case Studies
Subject heading(s):	Libraries, Children's—Budgets
	Libraries, Children's—California

275   "A Survey of Children's Librarians in Illinois Public Libraries" by Loriene Roy. *Library and Information Science Research* 9:187–211 (July-Sept. 1987).
Describes the educational preparation of children's librarians, as well as their job histories, present positions, career choices, and opportunities for advancement. Reports the suggestions of children's librarians regarding how administrators, the Illinois State Library, the

Illinois Library Association, and the American Library Association could help them.

Full report appears in the *Illinois Library Statistical Report, No. 21.* Springfield: Illinois State Library, 1986.

> Type of literature: Article—Research
> Funding source(s):   Illinois State Library
> Research method(s):   Questionnaire
> Subject heading(s):   Librarians, Children's—Illinois

276   "Survey of Children's Services" by the Area Children's Librarians Network. *New Jersey Libraries* 18:20–21 (Spring 1985).
Describes New Jersey library children's services in terms of age range of the clientele, book budget, access for children to all library materials, criteria for obtaining a library card, services offered, professional staffing, and lack of philosophy for library service to children in the state.

> Type of literature: Article—Research
> Research method(s):   Questionnaire
> Subject heading(s):   Libraries, Children's—Services—
>   New Jersey

277   "Survey of Children's Services in Missouri Public Libraries" by Patt Behler. *Show-Me Libraries* 32:14–16 (May 1981).
Describes the preparation for a statewide survey of children's services.

> Type of literature: Article—Research
> Subject heading(s):   Libraries, Children's—Services—
>   Missouri

278   *A Survey of Children's Services in Ohio Public Libraries 1979* by the Children's Services Survey Task Force. Columbus: Ohio Library Association, 1979. 62p. Appendix unpaged.
Describes Ohio public library children's services in terms of administration, staff, materials, facilities, programs, procedures, relationship with the community, and outreach programs. Concludes that the major problems were understaffing, underfunding, and assignment of other duties to the children's librarians.

> Type of literature: Report—Research
> Research method(s):   Questionnaire

Subject heading(s):   Libraries, Children's—Services—
                          Ohio

279 "A Survey of the Reactions of Nassau County (N.Y.) Librarians to the Proposition Made by the Commissioner's Committee on Library Development Concerning Children's Library Services" by Adele I. Friedman. Master's Thesis, Palmer
Graduate Library School, 1971. 41p.

Reports librarians' reactions to Commissioner Hacker's proposal that
school libraries assume responsibility for all library services to children. Although school librarians thought the plan had merit, half
of the school librarian respondents rejected the proposal, as did all
public school library respondents. Both types of librarians thought
that more complete services to children could be provided on a cooperative basis.

Type of literature: Master's Thesis
Research method(s):   Questionnaire
Subject heading(s):   School and Public Libraries

280 *Toronto Public Libraries: Goals, Objectives and Priorities* by the
Boys and Girls Services Task Force. Toronto: Toronto Public
Library, 1976. 75p.

Presents goals and objectives for the evaluation and selection of
materials, the role of the coordinator of boys' and girls' resources, the
relationship of school and public libraries, the role of professional
children's librarians, in-service training, the classification scheme
for children's materials, and interdepartmental relationships within
the branches. Provides specific recommendations for action on each
topic.

Type of literature: Policies
Subject heading(s):   Libraries, Children's—Goals and
                          Objectives—Toronto Public
                          Library

281 *Total Community Library Service*, ed. by Guy Garrison. Report
of a Conference Sponsored by the Joint Committee of the
American Library Association and the National Education
Association. Chicago: American Library Association, 1973.
LCCN 73-4310.

Includes (1) Kathleen Molz's "Past and Present Efforts at Coordination of Library Services at the Community Level," in which she highlights the trends in and studies about student use of libraries, and (2) Mildred Frary's comments identifying impediments to cooperation, including physical, political, fiscal, legal, and psychological barriers. Recommends actions for the sponsoring associations, for the federal government, for librarians, and for researchers.

Type of literature:	Conference Proceedings
Funding source(s):	J. Morris Jones-World Book Encyclopedia, ALA Goals Award Program
Subject heading(s):	Libraries, Children's—Conferences and Institutes—Proceedings
	School and Public Libraries—Cooperation

282 *Toward a National Program for Library and Information Services: Goals for Action* by the National Commission on Libraries and Information Science. Washington, D.C.: U.S. Government Printing Office, 1975. 106p. Stock number 052-003-00086-3.

Addresses the information needs of all ages and identifies the goals for a national program to provide every individual in the United States with equal opportunity of access to information resources that satisfy the individual's educational, working, cultural, and leisure-time needs and interests.

Type of literature:	Position Paper
Subject heading(s):	Libraries—Goals—United States

283 "Training for the Work of a Children's Librarian" by Anne Carroll Moore. *ALA Bulletin* 8:238–43 (July 1914).

Identifies topics to be used as a basis for preparing a thesis or for lectures in courses. Identifies skills needed by children's librarians.

Type of literature:	Article—Research
Research method(s):	Questionnaire
Subject heading(s):	Librarians, Children's—Education

284 *Tribal Library Procedures Manual* by Lotsee Patterson. Norman: School of Library Science, Oklahoma University, 1986. 112p. ED 278 527.

Provides guidelines for establishing a tribal library, including facility, collection, technical services, public services, and administration. Discusses the role of a children's librarian and the types of services to be offered.

Type of literature:	Guidelines
Funding source(s):	U.S. Department of Education, Office of Educational Research and Improvement of Library Programs
Subject heading(s):	Libraries, Tribal—Guidelines

285 *Urban Analysis for Branch Library System Planning* by Robert E. Coughlin, Françoise Taïeb, and Benjamin H. Stevens. Contributions in Librarianship and Information Science, no. 1. Westport, Conn.: Greenwood, 1970. 167p. ISBN 0-8371-5161-9. LCCN 71-133496.

Analyzes library usage in branch libraries and concludes that the socioeconomic level of residents in a service area is the most important factor determining the amount of use. Also concludes that bookstock is the next most important factor. Finds that the use rate by juveniles and young adults is higher than by adults. Identifies the effective service radius by socioeconomic level.

Type of literature:	Report—Research
Funding source(s):	U.S. Public Health Services Research Grant
Research method(s):	Questionnaire; Reports—Analysis
Subject heading(s):	Libraries—Branches
	Libraries, Children's—User Studies
	Philadelphia, Free Library of

286 "A View of Library Services Offered to Preschool Programs" by L. B. Woods and Bonilyn Hunt. *Top of the News* 36:368–74 (Summer 1980).

Examines the relationship of preschools to the public library through the study of a private nursery school, a private day-care center, a city day-care center, and a Head Start program. Reports a need for better communication among the schools and the library, especially in identifying the services of the library.

Type of literature:	Article—Research
Research method(s):	Interviews
Subject heading(s):	Libraries, Children's—Services
	Preschools

287   "Volume of Children's Work in the United States" by Arthur E. Bostwick. *ALA Bulletin* 7:287–91 (July 1913).

Identifies three stages in the development of services to children: (1) work with children; (2) the era of children's rooms; and (3) the era of the children's department. Notes that the Carnegie Library of Pittsburgh is the unique example of a library that began with all three stages at once. Cites dates for the three stages in other major libraries. Comments on the lack of professionally trained children's librarians and the lack of standardization of children's services.

Type of literature:	Article—Opinion
Subject heading(s):	Libraries, Children's—
	Administration and
	Organization
	Libraries, Children's—History

288   "We Hereby Resolve That Library Services to Youth Will Be a Part of WHCLIS II" by Bruce E. Daniels. *School Library Journal* 36:38–41 (April 1990).

Highlights the background and activities of the first White House Conference on Library and Information Services in 1979, noting that only seven resolutions dealt with children's services. Topics included free access to information, intellectual freedom, library instruction for children, full funding of the Elementary and Secondary Education Act, and specialists at the state library agencies. Identifies ways that youth librarians can use the second White House Conference as a means for strengthening youth services.

Type of literature:	Article—Opinion
Subject heading(s):	White House Conference on Li-
	brary and Information Services,
	Second

289   "What Am I Doing Here? or the Scope of Children's Services"
by Jane Campagna. *Illinois Libraries* 64:1177–79 (Dec. 1982).
Ascertains librarians' opinions regarding the scope of children's
services, whether children's services are overextended, and career
burnout. Finds concern about the low status of children's services
in terms of pay and the lack of opportunity to move up the professional ladder.

Type of literature:	Article—Research
Research method(s):	Questionnaire
Subject heading(s):	Attitude Studies
	Librarians, Children's—Illinois
	Libraries, Children's—Services— Illinois

290   *What Research Tells Us about Storyhours and Receptive Language*
by Frances A. Smardo, Principal Investigator, MIE Research
Project, and John F. Curry, Director, MIE Research Project.
Dallas Public Library and North Texas State University, 1982.
89p.
Examines the most effective of three types of story hour presentations ("live," video taped, 16mm film) on the receptive language
development (ability to comprehend language that is heard) of
preschool children of various socioeconomic levels.

Highlights of findings are reported in "The Effectiveness of Story
Presentation Methods upon Children's Receptive Language" by
Frances A. Smardo. *Public Libraries* 22:32–34 (Spring 1983).

Type of literature:	Report—Research
Funding source(s):	National Institute of Education
Research method(s):	Experimental
Research instruments:	Standardized *Test of Basic Experiences* (*TOBE*) 2, Revised Edition, Language Test, Level K (Prekindergarten and Kindergarten), CTB/McGraw Hill, 1978
Subject heading(s):	Children—Preschoolers
	Libraries, Children's—Programs and Activities

291   *What Should Libraries Do for Children? Parents, Librarians, and Teachers View Materials and Services in the South Central Regional System (Ontario)* by Adele M. Fasick. Research by Centre for Research in Librarianship, Faculty of Library Science, University of Toronto. Hamilton, Ontario: South Central Regional Library Board, 1978. 156p.

Surveys librarians and community members in the thirteen library systems in the Ontario region. Covers Canadian materials, nonprint materials, language materials, popular materials (series, comic books, games, toys), traditional services (materials, story hour programs, reading guidance for children and parents), services to preschoolers, school-related services, access to materials outside the library, social aspects of the library, and librarians' views of regional services. Concludes that a major weakness is that the patrons who use the libraries seem unaware of the depth and amount of materials and services available to children.

Type of literature:	Research—Report
Research method(s):	Questionnaire; Interviews
Statistical package:	Statistical Package for the Social Sciences
Subject heading(s):	Libraries, Children's—User Studies
	South Central Regional Library (Hamilton, Ontario, Canada)

292   "Where Are the Children's Librarians?" by Joyce Smothers. *New Jersey Libraries* 13:2–4 (Jan. 1981, Dec. 1989).

Reports on the responses of a questionnaire that appeared in the October 1980 issue of *New Jersey Libraries*. Responses indicated that children's librarians left their positions to seek opportunities for promotion, to earn more money than children's librarians ordinarily earn, because they had lost interest in the work, and for other reasons dealing with work conditions and family-related matters. Suggests that public library administrators can attract top-quality people to the field by giving higher priority to children's services.

Type of literature:	Article—Research
Research method(s):	Questionnaire
Subject heading(s):	Librarians, Children's

116

293   *White House Conference on Children in a Democracy, Prelimi-*
nary Statements: January 18–20, 1940, Washington, D.C., prepared for the use of the Report Committee, presented to
group meetings January 18, 1940, and revised in light of
suggestions received. Washington, D.C.: Superintendent of
Documents, n.d. 257p.

Concludes in the section "Specialized Library Service for Children"
(pages 135–43) that the United States should assist in the development of local public library service, provide financial aid for the
maintenance of such service, and provide traveling libraries to iso-
lated homes and communities. Recommends that libraries provide
collections and adequately trained personnel to serve children.

    Type of literature: Conference Proceedings
    Subject heading(s):   Libraries, Children's—
        Conferences and Institutes—
        Proceedings
        Libraries, State

294   *The White House Conference on Rural Education, October 3, 4,*
and 5, 1944. Washington, D.C.: National Education Association of the United States, n.d. 272p.

Finds one-third of the rural families without library facilities and
only 651 counties in the United States having county library service.
Recommends: "Rural children and adults need more library service.
Every rural community must consider how satisfactory service may
be obtained" (p. 190).

    Type of literature: Conference Proceedings
    Subject heading(s):   Libraries, Children's—
        Conferences and Institutes
        Libraries, Children's—Rural

295   "Who Speaks for the Children?" by Margaret Mary Kimmel.
School Library Journal 26:36–38 (Dec. 1979).

Describes changes in children's materials service delivery patterns,
relationships among professional groups, and the emphasis on serving "special" clients. Reviews sociological studies of occupations. Describes the author's dissertation dealing with professional and client
relationships, which tested the hypothesis that librarians who strive

more for professional recognition and status will have less regard for lower class and lower status clients. Reports that children's librarians had a lower opinion of their status than other public librarians.

Related entry: "Professional Striving and the Orientation of Public Librarians toward Lower Class Clients" (208).

Type of literature: Article—Research
Subject heading(s):   Librarians, Children's

296 "Wisconsin Public Library Service to Children: Its History and Development from 1872 to 1984" by Elizabeth Burr. *Wisconsin Library Bulletin* 79:138–46 (Winter 1984).

Highlights the contributions of individuals, agencies, and associations to the development of children's services. Describes the establishment of the Cooperative Children's Book Center, as well as service to children, including summer reading programs, story hours, and school libraries.

Type of literature: Article—Historical
Subject heading(s):   Libraries, Children's—History—
            Wisconsin

297 "The Year-Round Reading Program: An Experimental Alternative" by Penny S. Markey and Mary Kevin Moore. *Top of the News* 39:155–61 (Winter 1983).

Describes an experimental two-year pilot project at twenty-one community libraries in the Los Angeles County Public Library systems to test the feasibility of a year-round reading program. Reports that the study found that the year-round programs were attracting older readers (grades five through eight) who did not participate in the traditional summer reading programs.

Type of literature: Article—Research
Subject heading(s):   Libraries, Children's—Programs
            and Activities

298 "Youth Services Agenda for Illinois" by Carol J. Fox. *Illinois Libraries* 72:62–67 (Jan. 1990).

Provides goals, priorities, and time-lines as an agenda for youth services into the 1990s. The six goals are: (1) to reinforce the necessity, importance, and value of youth-oriented library work in the state of Illinois, (2) to enhance statewide resource sharing by including school, special, and academic libraries in the statewide automation programs, (3) to maintain, promote, and enhance existing reading and literacy programs for children and youth, (4) to develop and promote communication networks involving library youth services, (5) to promote staff development, continuing education, and certification, and (6) to identify and predict the needs of children and youth in Illinois that have an impact on library services.

Type of literature: Policy

Subject heading(s):   Libraries, Children's—Goals and Objectives—Illinois

Libraries, State—Illinois

Research Methods Used

Numbers after the headings indicate the entries in which the research method was used. This information is also provided after the descriptor "Research method(s):" in the bibliography entries. See the index for entries for Attitude Studies; and Libraries, Children's—User Studies.

Annual Reports—Analysis   101
Attendance Records—Analysis   104
Case Studies   145, 162, 185, 247, 268, 274
Children's Drawings—Analysis   134
Circulation Records—Analysis   36, 98
Collection Analysis   36, 64, 99, 241
Content Analysis   128, 197, 224, 266
Delphi   77, 119, 183
Experimental   65, 96, 192, 290
Historical Method   118, 129, 131, 180
Interviews   10, 13, 17, 20, 24, 28, 31, 36, 39, 49, 80, 97, 101, 114,
        134, 135, 146, 162, 170, 176, 178, 179, 185, 186, 193, 202, 220,
        224, 234, 248, 267, 272, 273, 286, 291
Job Announcements—Analysis   40, 41, 148
Observation   56, 146, 204
Output Measures   187, 188, 190
Quasi-experimental   56

Funding Sources

Numbers after the funding sources indicate the entries supported by those sources. This information is also provided after the descriptor "Funding source(s):" in the bibliographic entries.

American Library Association
    ALA Goals Award Program, J. Morris Jones-World Book Encyclopedia 281
    Library Extension Division 79
Baker and Taylor 24
Bush Institute for Child and Family Policy 274
California Library Association
    Children's Services Chapter 51
Carnegie Foundation 92, 169, 215
CLSI, Inc. 256
Council on Library Resources 159
    Fellowship 31
Dutton, E. P., John Macrea Award 261
Florida, State Library of 54
Gaylord Brothers, Inc. 256
Illinois State Library 108, 275
Indiana State Library 94, 167
Ingram Library Services 256
Michigan Educational Foundation 52

Type of Literature

Numbers after the headings refer to the appropriate entries. This information is also provided after the descriptor "Type of literature:" in the bibliographic entries.

Opinion   6, 109, 143, 155, 161, 165, 173, 175, 203, 206, 216, 217, 219, 239
Research   24, 49, 59, 77, 89, 169, 178, 215, 273, 285
Conference Proceedings   32, 35, 55, 174, 281, 293, 294
Directories   85, 121, 181, 252
Dissertations   7, 8, 10, 20, 33, 37, 40, 56, 62, 69, 74, 78, 84, 95, 96, 107, 118, 129, 145, 157, 179, 180, 208, 222, 247, 266, 269, 272
Essays   18, 168, 226
Historical   43
Opinion   30, 103, 116, 170
Guidelines   1, 50, 54, 60, 69, 72, 79, 112, 122, 123, 124, 125, 205, 209, 244, 284
Journals   149
Manuals   25, 45, 68, 102, 154, 189, 199
Master's Theses   9, 13, 66, 93, 98, 131, 176, 186, 204, 221, 261, 279
Policies   4, 22, 81, 136, 151, 153, 156, 212, 223, 245, 280, 298
Position Papers   194, 196, 240, 282
Reports   172, 211
Conferences   152
Demonstration Projects   127
Evaluation   141
Institutes   75, 105, 106, 120, 242
Opinion   110, 228
Planning   111, 164, 171, 201, 232
Research   11, 28, 31, 36, 51, 52, 57, 63, 88, 94, 99, 100, 101, 104, 113, 144, 146, 158, 159, 162, 167, 185, 187, 202, 233, 246, 267, 268, 270, 278, 285, 290, 291
Standards   21, 142, 165, 166, 177, 227, 242, 253, 254, 255, 256, 257, 258, 262, 263
Yearbooks   46

Index

Points of access are provided for authors, titles (italics), names of libraries, and subjects (capital letters) arranged alphabetically letter by letter; acronyms are interfiled. "A," "An," and "The," when the first words in titles, are omitted. Subtitles are not included unless they are needed to distinguish two or more works with similar titles. The numbers after the heading refer to the appropriate entries.

Example: "LIBRARIANS, CHILDREN'S—BIOGRAPHIES 12, 13, 20, 29, 147, 155, 179" refers to seven different entries (books, articles, and dissertations) that include biographical information.

Authors writing under more than one name are filed by the name used most frequently in the entries. A cross-reference from the less frequently used name is provided.

128

129

132

141

Phyllis Van Orden began her career as a children's librarian at the San Diego Public Library. She served as president of the Association for Library Service to Children in 1983–84 and chaired the 1989 Newbery Award Committee. Her books include *The Collection Program in Schools* (Libraries Unlimited, 1988). Now a professor at Wayne State University in library science, she completed this book, a Whitney-Carnegie Grant project, while on the faculty at the School of Library and Information Studies, Florida State University.